PAUL
The Work Entrusted

A Contemplative Journey Revealing Calling and Community

Dr. Cindy H. Carr, D.Min., MACL

This book is published by **CHC Connect**.

All views and opinions expressed in this work are those of the author. Any errors or omissions are unintentional.

Printed in the United States of America
First Edition, 2026

ISBN: 978-1-971192-35-2

For permissions or inquiries, contact:
Cindy H. Carr
cindyhcarr@outlook.com
www.cindyhcarr.com

How to Use This Book

This is a contemplative narrative—Scripture-adjacent, not Scripture-added. It stays anchored in Acts and Paul's letters while imaginatively entering the moments between the lines. Use it as a continuous read, or as a slow companion for prayer and formation.

The chapters in this book are first-person retellings rooted in Scripture. They follow the Biblical accounts of Paul's life and calling, while using imaginative detail to help you enter the story with your whole heart—mind, memory, fear, hope, and longing.

These narratives are not presented as verbatim Scripture, but as artistic renderings meant to illuminate what the text reveals: a life entrusted, formed through community, and lived one faithful step at a time.

Table of Contents

Chapter 1
Interrupted Zeal

When Calling Begins Before Understanding

(Paul tells his own story)

I was sure of myself. Not the casual certainty of a man who likes to argue—certainty with weight, like conviction had become bone.

I knew where the boundaries were. I knew what happened when people crossed them. And I believed it was my responsibility to guard what was sacred.

I didn't think of myself as violent. I thought of myself as faithful.

Purity mattered. Truth mattered. God's name mattered. And when I heard of a movement that sounded like danger—Messiah claimed by fishermen, holiness spoken in the language of mercy, sinners welcomed as if sin were small—I felt heat rise in me. Not fear. Duty.

That's how it begins, isn't it? The quiet belief that *you* are the one who must hold the line. That if you don't act, God will be dishonored. That restraint is weakness. That urgency is obedience.

So I went toward Damascus with letters in my hands and resolve in my chest. The road felt clean beneath my intentions. The sun was high. Dust clung to everything. My companions walked close enough that I could hear their breath and the scrape of sandals on stone.

The world felt normal.

Then the light came.

I wish I could describe it neatly. People want it to be tidy—a dramatic "moment" that fits in a frame. But it wasn't tidy.

It was interruption—pure, unavoidable, unstoppable.

It didn't feel like a spotlight. It felt like being found.

My body hit the ground before my mind could argue. The earth rushed up with a message I couldn't resist: *This is bigger than you.*

Then I heard my name—twice—spoken with a familiarity that hollowed me out.

"Saul. Saul."

And then: "Why are you persecuting Me?"

Me.

I had been persecuting *them*—that was my logic. I was correcting error. Protecting truth. Defending God. But the voice did not separate Himself from the people I had harmed.

He spoke as though every door I kicked in, every family I fractured, every trembling believer I dragged into daylight—He spoke as though I had laid my hands on *Him*.

Certainty leaves quickly when you realize you've been certain in the wrong direction.

I asked the only question that mattered—not as theology, but as survival.

"Who are You, Lord?"

And the answer came without explanation, without softening, without a map.

"I am Jesus."

The name I had treated as a problem was suddenly presence. Alive. Speaking. Addressing me. Stopping me.

And then—this still humbles me—He didn't give me a plan. He didn't hand me a platform to replace the harm I'd done. He didn't tell me how to make it right in a single speech.

He took my sight.

I opened my eyes and the world was gone.

If you've never been blind, you might think blindness is just darkness. But it's more than darkness. It's disorientation. Dependence. The loss of your ability to manage yourself. It is your life, suddenly out of your own hands.

The men around me led me by the hand. The man who came to seize others could not take a step unless someone guided him.

And this is where calling began—not when I saw a vision, but when I could not see at all.

God stopped my momentum. He shut the door on my certainty. And in the mercy of that closed door, He kept me from continuing to call my violence "obedience."

For three days I sat in the dark.

No applause. No clarity. No next step.

Just breath—too loud in the silence—and the slow, crushing realization that I had been wrong about the very thing I thought I understood best.

I fasted. Not as performance. There was no audience for that. I fasted because hunger matched my emptiness. Because food felt absurd when my whole life had been interrupted.

And prayer changed.

It stopped sounding like argument. It began sounding like surrender I didn't yet know how to offer.

Then I learned something that has shaped me ever since: while I sat there, undone, God spoke to someone else.

That detail matters.

Because we love calling stories that center the "called one." We love dramatic encounters. We love the voice from heaven.

But my calling didn't move forward through my courage.

It moved forward through someone else's obedience.

A man named Ananias.

He had every reason to fear me. He knew what I had done. He knew why I had come. And God told him to come anyway.

Community was stitched into my story before I could even name it as mercy.

I remember the sound of him entering—careful footsteps, a quiet inhale like he was steadying himself. I couldn't see his face. I couldn't read his expression. I couldn't control the moment. All I had was vulnerability.

Then he came close enough to touch me.

And he spoke the word I did not deserve:

"Brother."

Brother.

Not enemy. Not threat. Not monster.

Brother.

That single word did not erase what I had done. But it opened a door I could not open for myself: the possibility that my future wasn't only punishment—that God could offer mercy without denying truth.

He laid his hands on me and prayed. And something like scales fell from my eyes.

I could see again.

Walls. Light. Faces.

But the greater change wasn't my vision.

It was my understanding.

Calling is not God rewarding the impressive.

Calling is God entrusting a life.

And He entrusts it slowly—one faithful step at a time.

My first faithful step wasn't preaching. It was standing—still shaking, still humbled, still dependent—and receiving help from the very community I once tried to destroy.

That is how God began with me.

Not with a stage.

With a hand on my shoulder. With a brother's voice. With a closed door that became mercy.

With the kind of beginning you can only call grace.

Formation Pause

Pause here. Breathe slowly.

- Where have you been certain—and God interrupted you anyway?
- What might God be closing—not to punish you, but to protect you?
- Who has been an Ananias to you—someone whose obedience helped you begin again?
- If you are being asked to be Ananias for someone, what fear do you need to name honestly?

Pray one unedited sentence:
"Lord, entrust me with a faithful life—one step at a time."

Closing blessing:
May the God who interrupts us with mercy give you courage for the next faithful step. May Christ meet you in the dark places with kindness. May the Spirit weave community around you—hands and hearts that carry the work together.

Chapter 2
Brother

When Calling Requires Someone Else's Courage

(Ananias tells his own story)

I wish I could tell you I was brave the moment God spoke.

But obedience doesn't usually begin with courage.

It begins with a sentence that lands in your body like a warning.

"Ananias."

The voice was familiar—steady, unmistakable. The kind of familiarity that should have comforted me, except this time it carried weight, like God was about to ask for something that would cost more than convenience.

"Here I am, Lord," I said—because what else do you say when God calls your name?

Then He told me where to go.

"To the street called Straight."

An ordinary direction. Simple, even.

Then He told me who was there.

"Saul."

My stomach tightened before my mind could catch up.

Saul was the name we whispered. The name that made rooms go quiet. The name that made mothers pull children close. The name that made believers take the long way home.

Saul wasn't rumor.

Saul was a storm.

He was the one dragging people out. The one with papers. The one with authority. The one who called it righteousness while he shattered lives. We knew the stories. Some of us had lived them.

And now God was telling me to go to him.

Not to avoid him. Not to hide. Not to pray from a safe distance.

To go.

I argued the only way I knew how—honestly.

"Lord, I've heard from many about this man… how much evil he has done."

I needed to say it out loud. Fear grows in silence. It multiplies when you leave it unnamed.

"He has authority… to bind all who call on Your name."

I didn't add, *And I am one of them,* but it was there in my throat. I didn't say, *He could take me,* but it was there in my hands, suddenly weak.

God didn't shame my honesty.

He didn't say, Why are you afraid?

He said one word that did not erase the danger, but did redefine the moment:

"Go."

Not because Saul was safe.

Because God was sovereign.

"He is a chosen instrument of Mine…"

That word—*chosen*—caught in me at first. Not because I doubted God's mercy, but because I could still see the faces of the people Saul had harmed.

Then God added what my heart needed to hear:

"I will show him how much he must suffer for My name."

God was not excusing Saul.

God was confronting him—remaking him—from the inside out.

And suddenly I understood: calling sometimes looks like God reaching into the life of a dangerous man, not to endorse him, but to interrupt him. Not to reward him, but to reform him.

And still the command remained:

Go.

So I walked.

This is the part of the story people rush through.

But for me, it was the whole story.

Because the distance between God's command and my obedience wasn't theological.

It was physical.

Step. Step. Step.

Each footfall was a decision.

Normal life kept happening around me—faces in the street, sunlight on stone—while my insides felt like they were splitting.

There are moments when obedience feels like walking straight into the teeth of fear.

I found the house.

I stood outside the door longer than I like to admit. Not because I didn't believe God, but because my body didn't want to move.

Fear is not always a lack of faith.

Sometimes it's simply your nervous system telling the truth:

This could hurt you.

Then I knocked.

No thunder. No angelic escort.

Just a door and a decision.

When it opened, the air inside felt heavy—like waiting had pooled in the corners. Someone led me to the room where Saul was.

And there he was.

Not towering. Not shouting. Not commanding.

Sitting.

Still.

Blind.

I had expected a predator.

I found a man undone.

My fear didn't disappear. It changed shape.

Because it's one thing to fear someone powerful.

It's another thing to stand near someone broken and realize you now hold power in this moment—the power to harden or heal.

I could have kept distance and called it wisdom.

I could have spoken politely and left quickly.

I could have refused the word that would cost me the most.

But God hadn't asked me for the safe version of obedience.

He asked me to go near.

So I went near enough to touch him.

My hand hovered for a breath—one small pause where my heart said, *Are we really doing this?* Then I placed my hands on his shoulders.

His body tensed beneath my touch like someone expecting harm.

That detail has never left me.

Saul—the man who created fear—was braced for pain.

And then the word rose in me like a gift and a test at the same time.

"Brother."

Brother Saul.

I said it before I could talk myself out of it.

The word did not rewrite history. It did not erase what he had done. It did not declare him harmless.

But it opened a door.

Calling is full of doors like that—doors you don't want to open because you're afraid of what they will cost.

Doors that require you to treat someone as redeemable while you are still healing.

"Brother Saul," I said, "the Lord Jesus… has sent me so that you may regain your sight and be filled with the Holy Spirit."

I prayed as I touched him because prayer is where fear goes when it needs to become obedience.

Then it happened—something like scales fell from his eyes.

His breath caught. He lifted his head like he was learning light again.

He looked at me—no threat, no rage.

Just shock. Grief. Relief. Hunger.

A human being returning to himself.

He stood.

Still shaken. Still learning how to be led.

But standing.

And in that moment I understood something about community I had never understood so clearly:

Sometimes God entrusts a life into the hands of another believer first.

Not because the person called is ready.

But because they must receive belonging before they can live obedience.

Saul's calling did not begin with a sermon.

It began with someone risking a yes.

Mine.

That is sobering.

It is also holy.

Because it means calling is not private.

It is not a solo achievement.

It is not a platform for the impressive.

Calling is often a chain of ordinary obedience—one person responding, then another, then another—until a life begins to turn toward the work entrusted.

I left that house quieter than I entered it.

Not because the danger had been imaginary.

But because God had been God.

And God had asked me to be part of something I would not have chosen:

a new beginning for a man I would have rather avoided.

That's what community sometimes is—not comfort, but cooperation with grace.

Formation Pause

Pause here. Let the story settle.

- Where is God asking you to go nearer than feels comfortable?
- What fear do you need to name honestly before you can obey?
- Who has God asked you to call "brother" or "sister" when your instinct is distance?
- Is there someone's calling God wants to shape through your ordinary faithfulness?

Pray one unedited sentence:
"Lord, give me courage for the next faithful step—especially when it costs me."

Closing line:
Community is often the first place calling becomes real.

Chapter 3
Hidden and Held

When Calling Grows in Silence
(Paul tells his own story)

Chapter banner: After the light, after the fear, after the first brave "yes," I expected the road to open. Instead, the door of visibility closed. God did not waste the quiet.

Scripture anchors: Acts 9:30; Galatians 1:17–24; Acts 11:25–26; Philippians 3:7–11

I thought the interruption would be the hardest part.

The light.
The voice that knew my name.
The blindness that stripped me of speed, certainty, and control.

But the hardest part wasn't being stopped.

It was being *hidden*.

After Damascus, everything in me expected momentum. I assumed the next thing would come quickly—clarity, acceptance, a clean path forward. Surely the God who met me in blazing light would keep speaking in thunder.

Instead, the volume of my life turned down.

There were threats. Tension. Whispers that followed me like shadows. And in the middle of it, the community did something I didn't expect: they helped me leave.

Not because they doubted my sincerity.

Because my story had become combustible—dangerous to them, dangerous to me. In those early days, I was not yet safe enough to be visible, and the church was not yet strong enough to carry the weight of my name.

So they sent me away.

I didn't like it.

If I'm honest, it felt like being sidelined. Like God had started something dramatic and then tucked it into a drawer.

They took me to Caesarea.
Then to Tarsus.

Home, but not home. Familiar streets, unfamiliar soul.

Have you ever returned to a place that remembers the old you—while you are trying to learn the new you? The walls know your habits. The rhythms still fit your body. People speak your name as if nothing has changed.

But something has.

And you can't explain it without sounding strange.

That was me in Tarsus: a man newly undone, newly remade, still trying to understand what mercy had done to him.

I wanted to be useful. I wanted to prove something. I wanted to make up for the harm I had caused with visible, measurable good.

But God did not give me a stage.

He gave me time.

Time to lose my attachment to applause.
Time to have my motives sifted.
Time for the sharp edges of zeal to be softened into something steadier—something more like love.

This is what I've learned since:

A calling can be real and still be quiet.
A work can be entrusted and still be hidden.
A life can be chosen and still be waiting.

In those years, I carried questions that didn't have quick answers.

What do you do when you're called—but unseen?
What do you do when you're changed—but not yet trusted?
What do you do when the past is loud, and the future is unclear?

You learn the discipline of small faithfulness.

You learn how to pray without performing.
You learn how to obey without being noticed.
You learn how to be held by God when you cannot hold your own story together.

And then—quietly, unexpectedly—God sent help again through community.

Barnabas came.

That name still moves me, because it reminds me that God often advances a calling through someone else's kindness.

Barnabas didn't wait for me to prove myself publicly. He came looking. He remembered. He carried faith for me when my own faith felt like it had gone underground.

He found me and brought me to Antioch.

And Antioch was different.

Not polished. Not safe. Not uniform.

A city full of mixture—cultures and languages and questions. A place where the gospel wasn't an idea. It was a life shared across boundaries.

We stayed there a whole year.

A year of teaching.
A year of listening.
A year of watching God build a people.

And something happened to me in that year:

My calling stopped being a private story and began to become communal.

I was held by the prayers of others.
Shaped by the needs of others.
Strengthened by ordinary rhythm—day after day, meal after meal, worship after worship.

Calling isn't a platform. It's a life.

And sometimes the most significant step forward is the one no one applauds—the step only God sees, but heaven honors.

Formation Pause

Pause here. Breathe slowly.

- Where has God closed the door of visibility or speed in your life?
- What quiet season have you mistaken for being "set aside"?
- Who has been a Barnabas to you—someone who remembered you, found you, and called you forward?
- And who might God be asking you to go find?

Offer one quiet sentence:

"Lord, form me in the quiet, and teach me to be faithful in the next step."

Closing line:

Sometimes God hides a calling—not to reduce it, but to root it.

Chapter 4
Sent

When Calling Becomes Communal
(Paul tells his own story)

Chapter banner: Calling doesn't mature in isolation. Before I was "sent," I was held—by a gathered people, a steady rhythm, a Spirit who speaks in the middle of ordinary worship.

Scripture anchors: Acts 11:19–30; Acts 12:25; Acts 13:1–3; Galatians 2:1–2

Antioch taught me the shape of calling.

Not in a dramatic moment.
Not in a single sentence.
In the slow faithfulness of a community learning to love God together.

We gathered. We ate. We prayed. We taught. We listened. We kept showing up—especially on the days when nothing felt "special."

This is where many people misunderstand calling.

They think it's lightning.

But more often, it's weather.

A climate of obedience.
A steady temperature of love.
A repeated rhythm of worship that keeps forming you when you can't feel formation happening.

And Antioch did something else: it taught me that a calling is not only personal. It belongs, in some measure, to the people God has woven around you.

In those days, prophets came down from Jerusalem. One of them, Agabus, stood up and spoke about a coming famine.

And the church responded—not with panic, not with debate, but with generosity.

Each one gave what they could. Not for their own comfort, but for brothers and sisters they may never meet. They sent relief to Judea through Barnabas and me.

Do you see it?

Before I was sent with the gospel, I was sent with bread.

Before I was trusted to carry revelation, I was trusted to carry a gift.

Calling is often practiced in mercy long before it is expressed in mission.

Then time moved forward and trouble came again—this time through violence. Herod laid hands on the church. James was killed. Peter was imprisoned.

This is another part of calling people don't talk about enough:

Sometimes the very season you're being formed is also the season the world grows darker.

Suffering does not always mean you missed God. Opposition does not always mean you took a wrong turn.

Often it means the work entrusted is real.

Barnabas and I returned from Jerusalem, and we brought John Mark with us. More community. More story. More complexity. God wasn't giving me a clean, simple calling. He was giving me a life shared with people—people with strengths and weaknesses and learning curves.

Then came a day in Antioch that I will never forget.

We were worshiping. Fasting. Listening.

No spectacle. No shouting.

Just a gathered people doing the ordinary work of devotion.

And in the middle of that ordinary worship, the Holy Spirit spoke:

"Set apart for Me Barnabas and Saul for the work to which I have called them."

That was the moment of "sending," but notice how it happened:

Not in isolation.
Not in ambition.
Not in a private vision meant to make me feel special.

In community.

The church fasted again. They prayed. They laid hands on us. They released us.

I can still feel that moment—the weight of hands, the tenderness of blessing, the holy ache of being let go.

Sending isn't just a direction. It's a surrender.

It means you don't belong only to your own plans anymore.
It means you don't control the shape of your life the way you once tried to.
It means the Spirit gets to move you—sometimes into places you didn't request.

And I learned something critical:

Calling becomes communal when a praying people learns how to bless—and let go.

This is how the work entrusted moves forward.

Not as a stage. As a life.

A community.
A meal.
A year of staying.
A gift for the hungry.
A day of fasting.
A hand on the shoulder.
A door closing behind you.
And then—another step.

Formation Pause

Pause here. Breathe slowly.

- Where has God been forming your calling through ordinary community—people, rhythms, responsibilities?
- What "sending" is happening in your life right now—an invitation to release comfort, familiarity, or control?
- Who has laid hands on your life—through prayer, encouragement, advocacy, or quiet support?
- And who might God be asking you to bless and release?

Offer one quiet sentence:

"Spirit of God, teach me to listen, and give me courage to take the next faithful step."

Closing line:

Calling becomes communal when a praying people learns how to bless—and let go.

Chapter 5
The Sharp Disagreement

When Calling Includes Conflict

(Paul tells his own story)

Chapter banner: Some of the most formative steps I took were the ones that hurt—where trust frayed, voices rose, and two faithful people could not take the next step together.

Scripture anchors: Acts 13:13; Acts 15:36–41; Colossians 4:10; 2 Timothy 4:11

We didn't fight over theology.

That's what people assume—that conflict only counts if it's about doctrine. But some of the deepest tension comes from something more ordinary and more personal:

Who can I trust when the road gets hard again?
What kind of risk can I carry?
How do we move forward when we disagree about what wisdom looks like?

It began as a good idea.

"Let's go back," I said. "Let's visit the brothers and sisters in every city where we proclaimed the word of the Lord and see how they are."

I meant it—not as strategy, but as love. Because communities are not concepts. They are people. Names. Faces. Stories that keep unfolding long after you leave. And when you've watched the Spirit breathe life into someone's heart, you don't stop caring just because your itinerary changes.

Barnabas agreed. Of course he did. Barnabas was encouragement given flesh. He carried hope the way other men carry caution.

And then the fault line surfaced.

Barnabas wanted to take John Mark again.

I didn't.

Not because I hated him. Not because I needed to punish him. But because I remembered the moment he left us.

There is a kind of leaving that feels like betrayal when the work is hard and the danger is real. John Mark had turned back in Pamphylia. He had chosen home—or safety—or something he could not name—over the road we were walking.

Maybe he had his reasons. I'm sure he did.

But the memory of that departure stayed in me as a question:

What happens if the road collapses again—if prison comes again, if stones fly again, if hunger and sleepless nights return again—and he leaves again?

Barnabas saw a young man who needed restoration.

I saw a risk we could not afford.

And the disagreement sharpened.

That word—sharp—has weight. It means it wasn't a mild discussion. It wasn't a gentle "difference of opinion." It was tension with teeth. It was voices rising. It was trust trembling.

And for a moment, it felt unbearable—two men who had suffered together, prayed together, carried communities together… suddenly unable to agree on the next faithful step.

People want clean conflict. They want someone to be clearly right and someone to be clearly wrong.

But it didn't feel like that from the inside.

It felt like grief.

It felt like the ache of realizing that calling doesn't erase personality, history, or pain. The Spirit can unite hearts, yes—but we still have to do the human work of walking together, and sometimes that work breaks under strain.

In the end, Barnabas took Mark and sailed to Cyprus.

And I took Silas and went the other direction.

Two teams.

Two paths.

One gospel.

And still—if I'm honest—I mourned it.

Because even when God uses a split, it still costs something.

It costs the comfort of familiarity.
It costs the shared language of partnership.
It costs the easy trust you thought was settled.

And it exposes something humbling:

The work entrusted is bigger than my preferences.

I wish I could tell you I handled that moment with perfect grace. But the truth is, I carried a hardness for a while—hardness I called "discernment."

In my mind, it was wisdom. In my spirit, it was a wound that needed time and the Spirit's patient work.

Here is what I learned slowly, over years, not days:

Conflict does not automatically mean calling has failed.

Sometimes conflict reveals what still needs formation in us.

Sometimes it is the painful place where God shows us the difference between conviction and control, between zeal and love.

And sometimes—this matters—sometimes God redeems the very person you couldn't trust yet.

Because later, I wrote words I never would have expected to write.

I told the church to welcome Mark.

And near the end of my life, when I was cold and lonely and the road had finally worn my body thin, I asked for him:

"Get Mark and bring him with you, for he is very useful to me for ministry."

Useful.

Not disposable. Not disqualified. Useful.

That sentence is a mercy to me as much as it is to him.

Because it means God did not freeze us in our worst moment.

He kept working.

He kept healing.

He kept teaching me that people are not fixed. Not in failure. Not in fear. Not in immaturity.

And He kept teaching me something else:

Sometimes you can be right about the risk and still need to grow in tenderness.

Barnabas was not careless. He was compassionate.

And I was not evil. I was cautious.

But calling asked more of us than being "right."

Calling asked for love.

And love takes longer than we think.

If you are in a sharp disagreement right now—if a relationship in ministry, family, or community has frayed—do not rush to declare it meaningless.

Do not rush to call it proof you missed God.

Sometimes the Spirit is still present in the fracture, still at work in what you cannot yet mend.

Sometimes reconciliation is not immediate.

Sometimes it comes as a slow miracle—a heart softening, a story changing, a door opening again in a later season.

And sometimes the most faithful thing you can do is take the next step you can take without bitterness—trusting God to do what you cannot do right now.

Formation Pause
Pause here. Breathe slowly.

- Where has conflict revealed fear or control in you—disguised as "wisdom"?
- Who is the "Mark" in your story—someone you've quietly written off?
- Where might God be asking you to release the need to be right and choose the work of love?
- Is there a relationship you need to place back in God's hands—without forcing an outcome?

Offer one quiet sentence:
"Lord, soften what has hardened in me, and teach me how to take the next faithful step without bitterness."

Closing line:
God can use a fracture—and still heal what it cost.

Chapter 6
Closed Doors

When Calling Is Redirected

(Paul tells his own story)

Chapter banner: After conflict, I expected clarity. Instead, the Spirit led us by shutting doors—teaching me that guidance often comes first as a "no."

Scripture anchors: Acts 15:40; Acts 16:6–15; Proverbs 16:9; Romans 8:14

After the disagreement, I expected the road to feel obvious.

I assumed that once the decision was made—once Barnabas went one way and I went another—the Spirit would reward our obedience with smooth direction.

But calling doesn't work like that.

Sometimes the moment you think will bring clarity brings uncertainty instead.

Silas and I went through Syria and Cilicia, strengthening the churches. We did what we knew to do. We showed up where we were needed. We tended what had already been planted.

And then we tried to move forward.

We made plans. We picked routes. We chose what seemed wise.

And the Spirit said no.

We wanted to speak the word in Asia.

Forbidden.

We moved toward Bithynia.

Not allowed.

It's a strange thing—being called and still being stopped.

It's one thing to be blocked by opposition. You can make sense of that. You can name the enemy. You can brace yourself.

But it is another thing to be blocked by God.

No thunder.
No explanation.
Just a closed door.

And here is what that does to a soul:

It exposes how much of your peace is tied to progress.

How easily you equate forward movement with faithfulness.
How quickly you assume a "good plan" must be a God plan.
How often you believe you are safe as long as you can see the next step.

But the Spirit does not always guide us with a green light.

Sometimes He guides by restraint.

Sometimes He protects you from the very thing you would have called "success."

And in those days, I had to learn how to walk without the comfort of certainty.

We passed through region after region, not because we were wandering aimlessly, but because we were listening with our whole lives.

And listening is harder than planning.

Listening asks you to stay open.
To remain humble.
To keep moving without forcing direction.

Eventually we came down to Troas.

The sea air was sharp. The edge of the land felt like an ending. We had run out of obvious options.

And then, at last, the Spirit spoke differently.

A vision came in the night: a man of Macedonia, pleading, "Come over and help us."

It wasn't detailed. It wasn't a full strategy.

But it was enough.

And we concluded—together—that God had called us to preach the gospel there.

Do you see the pattern?

Closed doors, closed doors, closed doors—then a call.

No, no, no—then come.

God did not waste our restraint.

He used it.

He used it to direct us to people we would not have chosen if we had only followed our own preferences.

We sailed to Macedonia. We came to Philippi. And on the Sabbath we went outside the city gate to a place of prayer.

No synagogue full of eager listeners. No large crowd waiting.

Just a small gathering—women seated, hearts open, lives already hungry for God.

And there was Lydia.

A merchant. A worshiper. A woman with influence and a listening spirit.

As I spoke, something happened that I could not manufacture:

The Lord opened her heart.

That line matters to me.

Because it means the work entrusted was never finally dependent on my brilliance, my courage, or my ability to "break through."

God opens hearts.

I can show up. I can speak. I can serve. I can suffer. I can stay faithful.

But conversion—awakening—new birth—that is the Spirit's work.

And Lydia responded. She and her household were baptized. And then she did what the newly opened heart often does:

She made space.

She offered hospitality.

She insisted that we come and stay at her house.

And just like that, a closed door season became an open home.

Not a platform. A table.

Not a spotlight. A household.

This is how calling often advances:

Not by grand entrances, but by faithful listening.
Not by forcing doors open, but by following the Spirit's restraints.
Not by chasing the biggest opportunity, but by receiving the next assignment God gives.

If you are in a season of closed doors—if your plans keep failing, if your "good idea" keeps getting blocked—don't assume you are abandoned.

You may be being redirected.

And if you can't see where it's going yet, that doesn't mean God isn't leading.

It may mean He is teaching you the kind of trust that doesn't require explanation.

Sometimes guidance is a vision.

But often, it's a quiet "no" that becomes mercy later.

Formation Pause

Pause here. Breathe slowly.

- Where have you been pushing for an open door that the Spirit keeps closing?
- What "good plan" might God be restraining—not to punish you, but to redirect you?
- Where are you being asked to listen more deeply than you plan?
- What Lydia—what unexpected person, place, or household—might God be preparing as your next foothold?

Offer one quiet sentence:

"Holy Spirit, teach me to trust Your 'no,' and lead me into the work You have prepared."

Closing line:

Closed doors are sometimes the Spirit's kindness—guiding you toward the people you're meant to love.

Chapter 7
At Midnight

When Calling Is Tested in the Dark
(Paul tells his own story)

Chapter banner: Some truths can only be learned when there is no audience, no exit, and no immediate rescue—when faith must breathe in the dark.

Scripture anchors: Acts 16:16–34; 2 Corinthians 11:23–27; Psalm 42:8

We had followed the Spirit's leading into Macedonia.

Closed doors had brought us here.
A vision had confirmed it.
A household had opened its table.

By every measure I understood, we were finally "in the will of God."

And then trouble followed us.

It always seems to.

There was a young woman we encountered in Philippi—enslaved, exploited, used for profit under the name of "spiritual power." She followed us for days, shouting what sounded like truth but carried the weight of captivity.

At first, I endured it.

But there is a difference between patience and permission.

Eventually, I turned and spoke—not to her, but to the spirit that bound her. And in the name of Jesus Christ, she was freed.

What followed was not celebration.

It was rage.

Because when God liberates a person, He often threatens a system. And systems rarely release their grip quietly.

Her owners dragged us into the marketplace. Accusations flew. Truth bent under fear and economics. There was no careful investigation. No measured justice.

Just fists.
Rods.
Pain.

They beat us publicly. They stripped us of dignity. Then they threw us into prison and fastened our feet in stocks—positioned not for comfort, but for maximum strain.

I wish I could tell you I felt holy in that moment.

I didn't.

I felt bruised.
I felt confused.
I felt the familiar question rising again: *Did I misunderstand You, God?*

But something happens when you've walked with God long enough.

You stop demanding immediate explanation.

You learn how to stay.

Silas and I sat in the dark, backs burning, muscles trembling. The air was damp. The night stretched on.

And sometime around midnight—when the body is weakest and the mind most tempted to despair—we began to pray.

Not loudly.
Not dramatically.
Just honestly.

And then we sang.

Not because we were brave.

Not because we felt victorious.

But because something deeper than pain had been formed in us.

Worship had become muscle memory.

Trust had taken root below circumstance.

Other prisoners listened.

That detail matters.

Because calling is never only about you—even in suffering.

And then the ground shook.

Walls trembled. Doors flew open. Chains fell loose.

Freedom arrived suddenly, spectacularly.

But here's the moment that still surprises people:

We didn't run.

We stayed.

Because freedom isn't always about escape.

The jailer woke, panicked, ready to end his life—assuming the prisoners had fled and his future was over.

And I called out into the chaos:

"Do not harm yourself. We are all here."

The miracle wasn't just the earthquake.

It was restraint.

It was choosing presence over self-preservation.

That night, the jailer washed our wounds. We spoke of Jesus. His household believed. They were baptized before dawn.

And once again, calling unfolded in an unexpected way:

Through pain.
Through staying.
Through songs offered in the dark.

Here's what midnight taught me:

You don't sing *to* change the darkness.

You sing *because* the darkness cannot erase what God has already formed in you.

Calling is not proven by how quickly God rescues you.

It is revealed by what rises out of you when rescue hasn't come yet.

If you are in a midnight season—if you feel confined, misunderstood, or unjustly treated—don't assume God is absent.

He may be shaping a witness you could never choose.

Sometimes the deepest formation happens when the lights are out and the only thing you have left is trust.

Formation Pause
Pause here. Breathe slowly.

- Where are you being asked to remain faithful without immediate relief?
- What has God already formed in you that no circumstance can undo?
- Who might be listening to your life in this "midnight" season?
- What song—however quiet—could you offer tonight?

Offer one quiet sentence:
"God of the dark, remain with me, and teach me how to stay faithful here."

Closing line:
Midnight does not mean abandonment—it often means formation is going deeper.

Chapter 8
Received and Resisted

When Calling Isn't Welcome
(Paul tells his own story)

Chapter banner: In Thessalonica, obedience was met with hunger *and* hostility. Sometimes community protects a calling by sending you away—before you feel ready to leave.

Scripture anchors: Acts 17:1–15; 1 Thessalonians 2:1–12; 1 Thessalonians 3:1–5

Leaving Philippi, I carried two sounds in my body.

The first was the hymn—still lingering like smoke in my lungs, the memory of midnight worship echoing in places that had hurt. The second was the clank of chains, not because they were still on my wrists, but because some experiences stay with you even after the door opens.

Freedom is not always the absence of pain. Sometimes it is the presence of God *in* the pain, and the slow learning that you are not alone when you cannot control the outcome.

We walked west along the road, dust rising with each step. The world looked ordinary again—sky, stone, travelers passing without knowing what had happened in a prison at midnight. And I remember thinking, *Maybe the worst is behind us.*

It wasn't.

Thessalonica was a city with a pulse—busy, proud, awake. We arrived with bruises still tender, with our story still raw, with the gospel still burning in us like a secret we couldn't keep. There was a synagogue there, and as was my practice, I entered and reasoned from the Scriptures.

Three Sabbaths.

Three weeks of opening the story of God and saying what still startled people when spoken plainly:

The Messiah had to suffer.
The Messiah had to rise.
And Jesus is that Messiah.

Some listened.

Some believed.

Not all of them were Jews. That's the part that always disrupted the expected order—Greeks who had been standing at the edges of worship suddenly stepping in; women of prominence who had more to lose than many men and yet responded with courage; households rearranging their lives around a new center.

The gospel does that.

It moves through people you didn't expect and changes the shape of belonging.

For a moment, it felt like Philippi again—another open heart, another new beginning. And I remember the tenderness of those days: meals offered quietly, questions asked honestly, prayers shared in corners of homes where the world couldn't hear.

There is a kind of receiving that feels like mercy after suffering.

To be heard after being beaten.
To be welcomed after being accused.
To be given bread without suspicion.

But Thessalonica also taught me something harder:

The same message that heals some will threaten others.

The resistance didn't start as reasoned disagreement. It started as jealousy—an anger that someone else's influence was shifting. People who had been comfortable with the existing order felt it wobble, and fear disguised itself as righteousness.

They gathered troublemakers. They stirred the city. They turned public emotion into a weapon.

And once again, the gospel did not simply invite people into life—it exposed what was already sick beneath the surface.

They couldn't find us, so they found Jason—one of the believers who had taken us in. They dragged him and others before the authorities. They accused them of treason and chaos: "These men have turned the world upside down."

It's a strange thing, hearing truth spoken as accusation.

Because in one sense, yes—the gospel does turn the world upside down.

It takes the proud and calls them to humility.
It takes the powerful and calls them to servanthood.
It takes the outsider and calls them family.
It takes the cross and calls it victory.

But the accusation was meant to spark fear. It was meant to make the church in Thessalonica look dangerous. And the authorities, eager for control, required security—money paid like a warning: *Keep this quiet. Don't make trouble again.*

That's when the community did something that still humbles me.

They sent us away.

Not after a long debate. Not after waiting to see if it would calm down. That very night they moved quickly—because love sometimes looks like urgency.

They protected the church by removing the spark.

It is hard to be the spark.

It is hard to be the one who must leave for others to breathe.

And in that moment, I felt the ache of it: the unresolved conversations, the new believers still forming, the tenderness of a church just born—and now, separation.

People romanticize "mission," but sometimes mission feels like grief.

You don't always get closure.
You don't always get to finish what you started.
You don't always get to stay long enough to see stability.

You simply obey the next step.

So we went to Berea.

And something in Berea felt different immediately—not safer, exactly, but steadier. The people there listened with a kind of nobility, not because they were superior, but because they were willing to examine the Scriptures daily to see if what we said was true.

I loved that.

Not because it flattered me. Because it honored God.

Faith is not meant to be gullible. It's meant to be grounded.

And many believed—again, Jews and Greeks, women and men, people stepping out of old patterns into a new life.

But the shadow followed us.

The trouble in Thessalonica did not stay in Thessalonica. When they heard the word of God was being proclaimed in Berea, they came—agitating, stirring crowds, turning the air sharp with threat.

Here is something calling teaches you quickly:

Sometimes opposition is not a single event. It's a pattern.

You don't "get past it" like a chapter you close. You learn to live with it, to keep choosing obedience while the world pushes back.

And once again, the community did what love often does:

They protected me.

The believers sent me away to the sea.

Silas and Timothy stayed behind—for a time—to strengthen the church. But I was moved out of the city like precious cargo, escorted like someone whose presence carried danger.

I didn't like it. Not because I didn't trust them, but because it felt like weakness.

It is humbling to be protected.

To realize your calling is not only your responsibility—it is also your community's concern.

I traveled toward Athens alone.

And the solitude pressed in.

We don't talk enough about that part: the emotional cost of being separated from people you love, the ache of leaving believers mid-formation, the weight of carrying concern for churches that are still fragile.

In my letters later, you can hear it—the tenderness and the worry braided together.

To the Thessalonians, I wrote as a father and a mother at once: gentle and exhorting, affectionate and urgent. I reminded them that we didn't come with flattering speech or hidden motives. We didn't seek glory. We shared not only the gospel, but our own lives, because they had become dear to us.

That is what is rarely understood:

The gospel is not a product delivered efficiently.

It is a life shared.

And because it is a life shared, resistance hurts.

When the city rises against you, you don't only feel threatened. You feel grieved—because you love the people who are caught in the storm.

I also wrote something else—something I learned in my bones in seasons like Thessalonica and Berea:

We wanted to come to you again and again… but we were hindered.

Hindered.

Sometimes by human hostility. Sometimes by spiritual resistance. Sometimes by the necessary choices of wisdom and protection.

And in that hindrance, I learned a hard truth:

You can be faithful and still be blocked.

You can do the right thing and still be misunderstood.

You can preach the gospel and still be treated as danger.

Calling is not welcomed everywhere.

And yet—this is what kept me steady:

The work entrusted is not measured by how warmly it is received.

It is measured by obedience.

It is measured by love that keeps giving itself.

It is measured by perseverance.

I think about Jason sometimes—how he risked his home, his reputation, his safety. I think about the young believers in Thessalonica, learning how to follow Jesus under pressure. I think about the Bereans, searching Scripture daily with open hands. I think about the believers escorting me to the sea, knowing the danger, choosing care anyway.

And I think about the pattern that emerges across all of it:

God forms a people, and that people becomes both shelter and sending.

Sometimes you stay and build.

Sometimes you leave so others can stay.

Sometimes you are the one welcomed.

Sometimes you are the one resisted.

And through it all, the Spirit keeps doing what I cannot do:

Opening hearts.
Strengthening faith.
Anchoring believers in hope.

If calling is becoming costly for you—if your obedience is met with misunderstanding, if your faithfulness has stirred resistance—don't rush to interpret that as failure.

It may mean the gospel is actually doing what it does: revealing what is hungry and what is hardened.

And if you are in a season where others must protect you—where you must step back, move away, or be sent—receive that as grace.

Sometimes being sent away is not rejection.

It is preservation.

It is love.

It is the Spirit keeping the work entrusted alive until the next season comes.

Formation Pause

Pause here. Breathe slowly.

- Where has your obedience been met with resistance—not because you were wrong, but because the gospel disrupts what is comfortable?
- What community has sheltered you when your calling became costly?
- Where might God be asking you to leave—not in defeat, but in wisdom and protection?
- What would it look like to trust that God can strengthen what you cannot stay to finish?

Offer one quiet sentence:

"Lord, help me be faithful whether I am welcomed or resisted, and teach me to receive community as Your care."

Closing line:

Sometimes the Spirit protects the work entrusted by sending you away—so the gospel can remain and grow where you first planted it.

Chapter 9
Provoked and Patient

When Calling Learns the Language of a City

(Paul tells his own story)

Chapter banner: In Athens, my spirit burned—not only with grief at what was false, but with longing for what was possible. Calling sometimes requires you to speak truth without contempt, to engage a culture without losing your center.

Scripture anchors: Acts 17:16–34; 1 Corinthians 9:19–23; 1 Thessalonians 3:1–6

I arrived in Athens alone.

Not because I preferred solitude, but because sometimes the work entrusted moves in fragments—one person sent ahead, others delayed, the body of Christ stretched across distance.

Athens looked impressive.

Stone upon stone.
Beauty carved into permanence.
Ideas hanging in the air like incense.

It was the kind of city that made people feel small—and proud at the same time. The marketplace buzzed. Teachers gathered listeners as if wisdom were currency. And everywhere I turned, I saw altars, statues, temples—devotion made visible, worship made architectural.

Luke wrote that my spirit was provoked within me.

That's accurate.

But let me tell you what that provocation felt like.

It wasn't rage.

It was ache.

It was the grief of seeing people made for God spending their lives bowed to what cannot love them back.

It was the sorrow of realizing how easy it is for the human heart to trade the living God for something manageable—something beautiful, something familiar, something that doesn't demand surrender.

And yet, I didn't want to despise them.

Because I was not looking at strangers.

I was looking at people—made in God's image—reaching toward meaning the best way they knew how.

So I did what I always do.

I started where I could.

I reasoned in the synagogue. I spoke in the marketplace day by day with those who happened to be there. Not as a performer, but as a witness. Not trying to win arguments, but trying to tell the truth without breaking love.

Some philosophers listened—Epicureans and Stoics, men trained to dissect ideas like surgeons. They called me a babbler. They said I was preaching foreign deities—because I spoke of Jesus and the resurrection.

And then they brought me to the Areopagus.

A council. A platform. A place where ideas were weighed publicly.

It could have been the moment to prove myself.

To dominate.

To crush their assumptions with superior knowledge.

But calling does not mature through triumph.

It matures through faithfulness.

And faithfulness, in that place, required something specific:

Speak clearly.
Speak truly.
Speak humbly.

So I looked at what was already there.

I named what I could affirm.

"Athenians," I said, "I see that you are very religious."

That wasn't flattery. It was observation.

Their hunger was real.

Their searching was sincere, even if misdirected.

Then I told them about the altar I had found—an altar with words carved into it like a confession:

"To an unknown god."

That small altar was a doorway.

Not because ignorance is holy, but because humility is.

An admission of unknowing is sometimes the first step toward revelation.

So I said:

"What therefore you worship as unknown, this I proclaim to you."

And then I spoke of God—not as a concept, but as Creator.

The God who made the world and everything in it.
The Lord of heaven and earth.
Not contained by temples made with hands.
Not served as though He needed anything.

That mattered in Athens, because their gods were manageable—localized, contained, useful.

But the true God is not manageable.

He gives life and breath and everything.

He made from one man every nation. He set boundaries and seasons—not to control us like puppets, but so that we might seek Him, reach for Him, find Him.

And then I said the sentence that feels almost too tender to be true:

"He is not far from each one of us."

Not far.

Not hiding.

Not playing games with human longing.

Near.

I even quoted their poets.

Because truth is not afraid of language.

Because God has left fingerprints in more places than we expect.

"In him we live and move and have our being." "For we are indeed his offspring."

And then I did what calling always demands at some point:

I moved from affirmation to invitation.

From observation to repentance.

If we are God's offspring, then God is not gold or silver or stone. He is not a statue shaped by human imagination.

And I told them that God had overlooked times of ignorance, but now He commands all people everywhere to repent—because He has appointed a day to judge the world by a man He has raised from the dead.

That's where the atmosphere changed.

Because resurrection isn't just a comforting idea. It's a confrontation.

It means history is going somewhere.

It means the body matters.

It means death isn't final.

It means God has acted decisively in Jesus.

Some mocked.

Some said, "We will hear you again."

And some believed.

A few names are recorded—Dionysius, Damaris, others with them.

Not a mass revival. Not an obvious "success."

But a seed planted in hard soil.

And as I left the Areopagus, I carried something I have learned to carry often:

The ache of partial reception.

The strange humility of offering truth and watching it be refused by many.

The steady comfort of knowing the outcome does not define the obedience.

Here is what Athens taught me:

You can speak in love and still be dismissed.
You can contextualize without compromising and still be misunderstood.

You can tell the truth without contempt and still not "win."

Calling is not the art of convincing everyone.

It is the practice of being faithful to Jesus in front of whoever is listening.

Later I would write words that I learned in cities like this:

I became "all things to all people," not because I was changing the gospel, but because I was learning how to carry it across differences. I laid down rights. I adapted my approach. I listened. I studied the language of a place.

Not to blend in.

To reach.

Because love does that.

Love crosses.

Love learns.

Love speaks so the other can understand.

And still, love refuses to lie.

If you are standing in a place that feels like Athens—a workplace, a family system, a cultural moment where faith is treated like foolishness—do not assume your calling is invalid because people don't applaud.

You are not called to be impressive.

You are called to be faithful.

Your task is not to control response.

Your task is to bear witness with patience, clarity, and courage.

Some will mock.

Some will delay.

Some will believe.

And God will still be God.

He is not far from each one of us.

Formation Pause

Pause here. Breathe slowly.

- Where has your spirit been "provoked"—not into rage, but into grief and compassion?
- What "unknown god" do you see people serving today—success, image, control, pleasure, certainty?
- How can you speak truth in your context without contempt—and without compromise?
- Who is one person God may be inviting you to engage with patience rather than pressure?

Offer one quiet sentence:

"Lord, teach me to speak Your truth with love, and to trust You with the response."

Closing line:

Calling learns the language of a city—not to soften the gospel, but to carry it faithfully into human hunger.

Chapter 10
Staying in Corinth

When Calling Endures, One Day at a Time
(Paul tells his own story)

Chapter banner: In Corinth, God taught me the courage of staying—to work with my hands, to plant slowly, to keep speaking when I was afraid, to let community become steady enough to last.

Scripture anchors: Acts 18:1–18; 1 Corinthians 2:1–5; 1 Thessalonians 3:6–10; 2 Corinthians 12:9–10

Leaving Athens, I felt quieter than I expected.

Not defeated—just humbled. The city of ideas had taught me something I didn't want to learn: faithfulness does not always look like visible fruit. Sometimes you speak clearly, you love honestly, and only a few hearts open. And you still walk on.

So I walked on.

Corinth did not meet me with philosophy.

Corinth met me with noise.

A port city—money moving, bodies moving, languages colliding in the streets. Desire was not hidden here; it was advertised. People called it freedom. But as I watched, I could see how often "freedom" was simply hunger with no shepherd, appetite with no home.

And I was alone.

Silas and Timothy had not arrived yet. The absence pressed on me in places I could not name. Calling can sound heroic in a retelling. In real time it often feels like stepping into a city you didn't choose, carrying a promise you cannot prove, and asking your own trembling heart to keep going.

So I did what I could do.

I looked for work.

Not because preaching didn't matter—because it did. But because I had learned something about stewardship: the gospel is offered freely. And sometimes the most faithful way to guard that freedom is to refuse to turn it into a transaction.

That is how I found them.

Aquila and Priscilla.

Displaced, like so many are displaced—moved by an emperor's decree, uprooted without warning, forced to rebuild life in a new city with unfamiliar streets. They made tents.

Leather. Thread. Needle. Long hours.

Ordinary labor.

The kind of labor that does not ask the world to notice it.

I stayed with them because we shared the same trade. And in their home I felt something I hadn't expected to feel so quickly in Corinth:

steadiness.

It is a strange mercy when God gives you a table before He gives you a platform. When He gives you companionship before He gives you momentum. When He reminds you that calling is not only carried by proclamation—it is carried by presence.

Day after day my hands learned the rhythm of work again.

Work has its own quiet discipline. It brings you back to reality. It humbles the parts of you that want to live on adrenaline. It teaches you to keep showing up when the day is unremarkable. There is holiness in that kind of life—not because tents are sacred, but because obedience often begins as simple endurance.

And on Sabbaths, I went to the synagogue.

I reasoned. I persuaded. I kept opening the Scriptures and saying, as plainly as I could: Jesus is the Messiah.

Some listened.

Some resisted.

Some hardened.

The tension rose until words began to land like stones. And I felt an old impulse in my chest—fight harder, prove more, sharpen the argument, win.

But I had already learned what zeal can become when it is not shaped by love.

So when opposition settled into stubborn refusal, I set a boundary. I shook out my garments—not as contempt, but as clarity. And I turned toward the Gentiles.

That wasn't abandonment.

It was direction.

The gospel was moving toward those ready to receive it.

A man named Titius Justus opened his home—right next door to the synagogue. Again it was a door. Again it was a table. Again it was ordinary hospitality making room for extraordinary grace.

Then Crispus believed—the ruler of the synagogue—along with his household.

Others believed too.

They were baptized.

And slowly, like something tender pushing through harsh soil, a community began to form.

But I need to tell you the part people tend to skip.

I was afraid.

Not the kind of fear that makes you run immediately.

The kind that settles in your bones when you realize the cost will keep coming.

Corinth was not gentle.

It could swallow a new believer and call it normal. It could tempt people back into old patterns with a thousand small invitations. And I carried the weariness of many roads—the accusations, the beatings, the constant need to start again.

I wanted this community to survive.

I wanted the gospel to take root deeply enough that when I left, they would still stand.

And yet, I could feel my own limits.

There is a fatigue that comes not from one hard moment, but from repeated courage.

From always having to begin again.

From always being the stranger.

From always having to trust God in another unfamiliar place.

Then one night, the Lord spoke to me in a vision.

Not with a strategy.

With presence.

"Do not be afraid… go on speaking… do not be silent… I am with you… I have many in this city who are My people."

Many.

That word steadied me like a hand on my shoulder.

Because when you walk through a city like Corinth, all you can see at first is darkness—idols, appetite, exploitation, restless longing. You can forget that God sees hidden hearts.

God sees future brothers and sisters before you can name them.

God is already at work in places that look unlikely.

So I stayed.

A year and six months.

Not touring.

Not chasing the next city.

Staying.

Teaching.

Eating.

Listening.

Learning their names, their histories, their wounds.

Watching the Spirit form a people out of an unlikely mixture—different backgrounds, different stories, different kinds of brokenness, all learning how to belong to Jesus in a place that tried to own them.

Staying taught me something I did not learn on the road:

sometimes calling is proved not by how far you travel,
but by whether you can remain.

Whether you can answer the same questions again without irritation.

Whether you can correct patterns patiently.

Whether you can love people who are still messy and immature and sincerely trying.

Whether you can keep showing up when the work is slow.

When Silas and Timothy finally arrived, they brought news from Macedonia—and something in me softened with relief.

The Thessalonians were standing firm.

The fragile community I had left in the night was still breathing, still believing, still loving.

Do you know what that does to a weary heart?

It gives you courage you didn't know you needed.

Because one of the hidden burdens of calling is carrying concern for people you cannot see.

And then Corinth tested us again.

Accusations.

A unified attack.

A tribunal.

I prepared to speak—to defend, to reason, to explain.

But Gallio dismissed the case. He refused to be used as a tool for religious violence. He drove them away from the judgment seat, and the threat dissolved into public confusion.

Sometimes God protects the work entrusted in ways that don't feel spiritual at all.

A Roman official's impatience.

A case thrown out.

Bureaucratic indifference that becomes mercy.

And again I remembered:

this life is not held by my strength alone.

It is held by God—through community, through providence, through unexpected shields I did not arrange.

Later, when I wrote to the Corinthians, I remembered how I first came to them:

in weakness, in fear, in much trembling.

Not as a confession of failure, but as a testimony of grace.

Because the power was never in my confidence.

The power was in God.

"My grace is sufficient for you, for My power is made perfect in weakness."

That is not a verse you quote when you want to sound spiritual.

It is a sentence you cling to when you are tired and still called.

Calling isn't a platform.

It's a life.

And in Corinth, the life entrusted to me looked like this:

hands that worked,
a mouth that kept speaking,
a heart that kept staying—
one ordinary day at a time—
until community became steady enough to last.

Formation Pause

Pause here. Breathe slowly.

- Where is God inviting you to practice the courage of staying—showing up again, being faithful again, loving again, even when the work feels slow?
- Are you in a season where your calling feels ordinary—work, routine, small conversations—and you're tempted to believe it "doesn't count"?
- What fear is trying to make you silent, and what would it look like to keep speaking with humility and steadiness?
- Who has strengthened your endurance simply by standing firm—without fanfare?

Offer one quiet sentence:

"Lord, teach me the courage of staying—one faithful day at a time."

Closing line:

Sometimes the most courageous obedience is not the next city—it's the next day.

Chapter 11
Hands and Hearts

When Calling Builds What It Needs

(Paul tells his own story)

Chapter banner: Over time, calling is held up by unseen labor—hands that serve, homes that open, gifts that strengthen the weak, and leaders who learn to stay tender while the work grows.

Scripture anchors: Acts 18:18–28; Acts 19:1–10; 1 Corinthians 3:5–9; 1 Corinthians 16:19; Romans 16:3–4

After Corinth, the road did not become easier.

It became wider.

When you stay long enough in one place to watch a community form, you begin to see what the work actually requires. Not only preaching. Not only courage. Not only endurance.

It requires people.

And not just "people who attend." People who carry weight. People who open their homes. People who teach quietly. People who absorb risk. People who do the unglamorous work that keeps a church from becoming a moment and turns it into a life.

Leaving Corinth, I carried gratitude—and I carried fatigue.

I had stayed a long time. I had watched the gospel take root in difficult soil. And I knew I couldn't stay forever, even when part of me wanted to. There is always another city. Another need. Another invitation that pulls at the edges of your life.

So I left.

Not to escape.

To obey.

On the way, I traveled with Priscilla and Aquila—friends given by God, steady companions whose faithfulness had already shaped more than they knew. They understood labor. They understood displacement. They understood what it meant to rebuild.

And as we moved, I realized something: the work entrusted was no longer carried only by my voice.

It was being carried by hands and hearts I could trust.

We came to Ephesus.

A city that felt like a crossroads—ideas, commerce, religion, power all colliding. Not a quiet place. Not a simple place. But a place where hunger and darkness lived close together.

I entered the synagogue, as I often did, and reasoned with the Jews there. They asked me to stay longer. That request was a gift. Sometimes people resist; sometimes they lean in. Sometimes a door opens and you feel it.

But I did not stay.

Not because Ephesus didn't matter. Because I was learning something about timing: you can love a door and still know it isn't yours to walk through yet.

I promised, "I will return to you if God wills."

And I left Priscilla and Aquila there.

That detail matters.

Because it means the gospel didn't leave Ephesus when I did.

It stayed.

In a couple's home.
In their conversations.
In their hospitality.
In their steady presence.

This is how God often builds what He needs:

Not with spectacle.

With people.

While I was gone, another man arrived in Ephesus—Apollos. A gifted speaker. Fluent, knowledgeable, passionate. He spoke boldly about Jesus, but his understanding was incomplete. He knew the baptism of John, the preparation, the call to repentance. But he needed the fuller story—the Spirit's work, the breadth of grace, the life of Jesus unfolding beyond the doorway of beginnings.

And this is where you see the beauty of quiet leadership.

Priscilla and Aquila listened to him.

They didn't shame him in public. They didn't compete for influence. They didn't correct him to prove they were right.

They took him aside.

And they explained the way of God more accurately.

There's a tenderness in that—an integrity that refuses to turn formation into humiliation.

It takes strength to correct without crushing.

It takes love to build someone up without needing credit.

Apollos received it.

And later he became a powerful encouragement to believers elsewhere—watering what others had planted, strengthening what had already begun.

That's the work of hands and hearts again:

Truth carried through relationship.

Growth offered through humility.

Community protecting the beauty of learning.

When I finally returned to Ephesus, I encountered another sign that calling is rarely simple.

I met some disciples—men who were sincere, responsive, hungry. But as we spoke, it became clear they hadn't received the fullness of what God was doing. They had been baptized into John's baptism—repentance, preparation, longing.

But they hadn't heard about the Holy Spirit.

So we talked.

Not as a debate, but as an opening.

We spoke of Jesus—of the One John pointed to. And they were baptized in the name of the Lord Jesus.

Then I laid my hands on them and prayed.

And the Holy Spirit came.

Not because I had power in my hands. Because God keeps His promise to fill those who turn toward Him.

And that moment taught me something I still return to:

There is a difference between being corrected and being filled.

A difference between information and transformation.

You can know true words and still lack strength to live them.
You can have sincere faith and still need deeper grounding.
You can belong to God and still need to receive what God has always intended to give—His Spirit, His presence, His power for the long road.

After that, I returned to the synagogue and spoke boldly for months—reasoning, persuading, calling people toward the kingdom of God.

Some believed.

Some resisted.

Some grew hard, and they began to speak evil of the Way publicly.

And when it became clear that the synagogue could no longer hold the weight of what was happening, I did something I have learned to do without bitterness:

I moved the work.

Not away from people, but toward those ready to learn.

We withdrew and began meeting in the hall of Tyrannus.

A rented space. A public room. Ordinary walls. No sacred architecture. No religious prestige. Just a place where people could gather and be formed.

Day after day.

Not once a week with polite distance, but with repeated, steady exposure to the story of God.

And something happened in Ephesus that I want you to notice:

The work multiplied through consistency.

Through teaching that was not flashy but faithful.
Through questions asked and answered.
Through lives being reordered slowly.
Through a community learning to exist in a city full of competing gods.

Over time, the word spread widely—so widely that it began to touch not only individuals but the atmosphere of the region.

This is how the gospel moves when it matures:

Not always with a single dramatic event, but with accumulated faithfulness.

And in the center of that faithfulness were people.

Not just me.

Aquila and Priscilla, opening their home again and again.
Apollos, strengthened and sent.
Disciples growing into leaders.
Believers learning to carry one another's burdens in a city that taught them to carry only themselves.

Later, when I wrote about the church, I reached for agricultural language because it fit what I had lived:

"I planted. Apollos watered. But God gave the growth."

That sentence keeps me humble.

Because it means I am not the source.

I am not the savior.

I am not the center.

Calling is not God building a platform for one person.

Calling is God forming a people.

And when God forms a people, He uses many hands.

Many hearts.

Different gifts.

Different temperaments.

Different kinds of courage.

Some preach.
Some teach.
Some protect.
Some host.
Some give.
Some correct gently.
Some labor unseen.
Some simply endure.

And God gives growth.

If you've been tempted to believe your calling only counts if it is visible, let Ephesus correct you.

If you've been tempted to believe you must do everything alone, let Priscilla and Aquila remind you:

The gospel often travels through the faithfulness of a household.

If you've been tempted to believe correction must be harsh to be true, let their gentle instruction of Apollos remind you:

Love can be accurate.

And if you've been tempted to measure success by speed or spectacle, let the hall of Tyrannus remind you:

Formation often looks like daily faithfulness in an ordinary room.

This is the kind of work that lasts.

Not because it is flawless.

Because it is shared.

Because it is rooted in love.

Because it is built by hands and hearts surrendered to the same Lord.

Formation Pause

Pause here. Breathe slowly.

- Who are the "hands and hearts" God has woven into your calling—people who support, strengthen, correct, or carry the work with you?
- Where have you been trying to do alone what God intends to build as a community?
- Is there a place in your life where you need both truth *and* tenderness—more accurate instruction without shame?
- What "ordinary room" has God given you for formation—an unglamorous place where faithfulness can grow day after day?

Offer one quiet sentence:

"Lord, teach me to receive community as Your gift, and to build with others in humility and love."

Closing line:

God gives growth—but He often grows it through ordinary hands, faithful hearts, and a people willing to share the work entrusted.

Chapter 12
Power and Pressure

When Calling Collides With the Unseen and the Crowd

(Paul tells his own story)

Chapter banner: In Ephesus, I learned that spiritual power is not a performance—and that when the gospel confronts unseen darkness, it also threatens visible economies. Sometimes calling provokes a public storm.

Scripture anchors: Acts 19:11–41; 1 Corinthians 15:9–10; Ephesians 6:10–12

Ephesus was not just a city.

It was an atmosphere.

It carried beauty and commerce and learning, but it also carried something heavier—devotion woven into business, spirituality packaged for profit, fear disguised as religion. People didn't simply believe in gods here. They depended on them. Their livelihoods were braided into worship.

And when the gospel begins to take root in a place like that, it does not remain private for long.

For a while, the work felt steady.

We taught daily. We listened. We answered questions. We watched lives reorient slowly—families changing, habits shifting, loyalties moving from the old gods to Jesus. It wasn't dramatic every day. Mostly it was quiet and persistent, like water wearing a path through stone.

But then something changed.

Not because I became more impressive.

Because God began to display His mercy in ways that people couldn't ignore.

Luke later wrote that God did extraordinary miracles by my hands.

That phrase makes me uncomfortable if you read it the wrong way.

Not because miracles aren't real—but because the human heart is quick to turn power into personality.

So let me say it plainly:

It wasn't my hands.

It was God's kindness.

Even cloth that had touched my skin—handkerchiefs, aprons from work—were carried to the sick, and people were healed. Those oppressed by unclean spirits were set free.

And I watched it all with awe and caution.

Awe, because God was liberating people.
Caution, because crowds love outcomes more than they love Jesus.

Power attracts imitation.

And imitation is where things got dangerous.

There were some itinerant Jewish exorcists—men who traveled using spiritual language like a tool. They watched what God was doing and tried to copy it.

Not to worship Jesus.

To leverage His name.

They spoke into a demonized man: "I adjure you by the Jesus whom Paul proclaims."

But the spirit answered them in a way that still sobers me:

"Jesus I know, and Paul I recognize, but who are you?"

Then the man leapt on them with such violence that they fled wounded and naked.

It spread quickly through the city—fear and fascination braided together.

And here is what that moment revealed:

The name of Jesus is not a charm.

It is not a technique.

It is not a borrowed phrase you can use without surrender.

Authority is not a performance.

It is relationship.

It is belonging.

It is the difference between speaking about Jesus and living under His lordship.

And as fear moved through Ephesus, something else happened—something beautiful:

Many who had believed came confessing and divulging their practices.

Not because they were shamed into it.

Because light was reaching places they had kept hidden.

People brought their magic books—expensive, treasured, identity-defining—and burned them publicly. The cost was immense. The loss was real. But something stronger than loss was happening:

Freedom.

This is what I learned watching those fires:

Repentance is not only turning away from sin.

It is also letting go of false power.

It is the surrender of control.

It is the decision to stop trying to manage the spiritual world with techniques, and instead trust the living God with your life.

And the word of the Lord continued to increase and prevail.

Prevail.

Not because we argued louder.

But because people surrendered deeper.

Not because I performed well.

Because Jesus was Lord.

That kind of movement never stays hidden.

When enough people leave behind old devotions, the economy notices.

In Ephesus, the temple of Artemis wasn't just a religious center. It was an identity. A pride. A public symbol. Craftsmen made shrines—silver images sold to pilgrims. Their income depended on worship continuing as usual.

So when the gospel started disrupting usual worship, fear rose—not fear of theological error, but fear of financial loss.

A man named Demetrius gathered the craftsmen and spoke skillfully.

He framed the gospel as a threat to Artemis. He appealed to pride, to tradition, to the city's reputation. He stirred the kind of anger that feels righteous because it is shared.

Soon the whole city was in confusion.

People rushed into the theater—thousands shouting, bodies pressed together, emotions multiplying. They seized Gaius and Aristarchus, my companions.

And something in me surged.

I wanted to go in.

Not to be a hero.

To stand with them.

But the disciples wouldn't let me.

Friends held me back. Even some officials—Asiarchs who had become friendly—sent word urging me not to venture into the theater.

Not because I was a coward.

Because wisdom is sometimes restraint.

Because courage is not always movement.

Because some battles are not yours to fight with your body.

So I stayed back, trembling with helplessness, listening to the roar.

For two hours they shouted:

"Great is Artemis of the Ephesians!"

Two hours.

Do you know what a crowd can become in two hours?

A crowd becomes its own god.

Reason disappears. Individual conscience dissolves. The chant becomes identity.

And in the middle of that, a city clerk—an ordinary official—finally quieted the people.

He appealed to law. To procedure. To the danger of being charged with rioting. And slowly, the roar drained out of the theater like water returning to its channel.

Not because Artemis was vindicated, but because order reasserted itself.

And the crowd dispersed.

That day taught me what I wish every believer understood early:

Our struggle is not only with people.

It is with powers.

With principalities.

With forces that manipulate fear, profit, pride, and devotion.

Flesh and blood are never the deepest enemy.

They are often the battlefield.

So we do not wage war the way the world does.

We do not match rage with rage.

We do not sanctify chaos.

We do not use Jesus' name as a weapon to win a cultural argument.

We remain steady.

We stay surrendered.

We speak truth without becoming brutal.

And we trust that Jesus is Lord even when a city shouts a different confession.

Ephesus also taught me something tender:

Community saves lives.

Gaius and Aristarchus were not abandoned. We endured together.

The disciples held me back, not to silence me, but to protect the work entrusted. They understood something I didn't want to accept in the moment: sometimes the most faithful action is not advancing into danger—it is remaining alive to serve another day.

Calling isn't proved by recklessness.

It's proved by obedience.

And obedience sometimes looks like restraint, like listening to wise friends, like letting the Spirit teach you humility through limitation.

If you are in a season where spiritual pressure feels intense—where conflict is more than interpersonal, where fear is thicker than logic—remember this:

The name of Jesus is not a tool.

It is a refuge.

And the power of God is not given so you can look impressive.

It is given so you can endure, resist evil, and keep loving in a world that wants to turn everything into a spectacle.

If your calling has provoked opposition, that does not automatically mean you've made a mistake.

It may mean the gospel is touching something real—something entrenched, something profitable, something defended by crowds.

Stay steady.

Let community hold you.

Do not confuse noise with authority.

Jesus is Lord even when a city chants another name.

Formation Pause

Pause here. Breathe slowly.

- Where have you been tempted to treat Jesus' name like a technique—something to use rather than Someone to trust?
- What "false power" might God be inviting you to release—control, superstition, image management, spiritual performance?
- Where is your calling colliding with systems—habits, economies, expectations—that don't want to change?
- Who are the wise friends holding you back from reckless courage—and can you receive that restraint as love?

Offer one quiet sentence:

"Lord Jesus, keep me surrendered in the storm, and teach me to trust Your authority without striving."

Closing line:

When the gospel confronts unseen darkness, it often stirs visible crowds—but Jesus remains Lord, and the work entrusted continues through steady, surrendered faithfulness.

Chapter 13
The Weight of Farewell

When Calling Must Speak Tenderly and Leave Well

(Paul tells his own story)

Chapter banner: There are seasons when calling feels like motion—cities, roads, open doors. And then there are moments when calling feels like farewell: telling the truth with tears, blessing what you cannot control, and leaving people in God's hands.

Scripture anchors: Acts 20:1–38; 2 Corinthians 2:1–4; 1 Thessalonians 2:7–12

After Ephesus, I carried two kinds of weight.

One was external—the usual strain of travel, the planning, the responsibilities that never stopped multiplying. The other was internal: the knowledge that love makes you vulnerable.

You cannot stay with people, teach them, eat at their tables, watch their lives change, and remain untouched.

You leave pieces of yourself behind.

I traveled through Macedonia, encouraging the believers. I spoke many words—Luke says it that way, and it's true. Because sometimes encouragement cannot be rushed. Sometimes it takes time to remind people of what is true when the world is loud and the heart is tired.

Then I went to Greece and stayed three months.

And even there—resting, teaching, strengthening—danger still found me. A plot formed against me. The road shifted again. Plans changed, not because I was indecisive, but because calling often requires flexibility that feels like surrender.

So I returned through Macedonia.

That pattern kept repeating: go, be hindered, go another way, keep going.

Eventually we came to Troas.

Troas was meant to be a brief stop. A place to gather with the believers before moving on. But even brief stops become holy when love is present.

We met on the first day of the week to break bread.

The room was crowded—people pressed in, lamps burning, air heavy with warmth. We talked late into the night, because goodbyes create urgency. When you know you're leaving, words become precious. You stop wasting them.

A young man named Eutychus sat in the window.

He grew sleepy.

He fell.

Three stories down.

The kind of moment that makes a room go silent in a single breath.

We ran down. We held him. And by God's mercy, he lived.

People call it a miracle—and it was. But for me it was also a parable:

Life is fragile.

Community matters.

And sometimes grace meets you exactly where you fall.

We went back upstairs, broke bread, talked until daybreak.

Then we left.

From Troas, I traveled toward Jerusalem, but I avoided returning to Ephesus.

Not because I didn't love them.

Because if I saw them again, I might not leave.

There are goodbyes that weaken your resolve, and I knew my heart.

So I sent for the elders to meet me at Miletus.

When they arrived, I looked at their faces and felt the familiar ache: these were not coworkers. They were beloved. Men who had carried weight with me, who had watched the word of God spread through ordinary days, who had endured the uproar, the pressure, the confusion.

And now I had to speak plainly.

I reminded them how I lived among them—serving the Lord with humility and tears, enduring trials, not shrinking back from declaring what was profitable, teaching publicly and from house to house.

That phrase matters: **tears**.

Because calling is not always strong in the way people imagine.

It is not always composed and fearless.

Sometimes it is a man preaching with a throat tight with grief because love is real and the future is uncertain.

Then I told them what they didn't want to hear.

I was going to Jerusalem—bound in spirit. Not fully knowing what would happen, only knowing that afflictions and imprisonment waited for me.

I could feel their alarm.

I could see it in their eyes: *Don't go.*

And this is where calling becomes very personal.

Because in moments like that, you feel the tension between two loves:

Love for the people you want to stay with,
and love for the obedience you must not abandon.

I said the words as truth, not bravado:

"I do not account my life of any value nor as precious to myself, if only I may finish my course and the ministry I received from the Lord Jesus."

That doesn't mean I didn't value life.

It means the work entrusted was bigger than my comfort.

Then I spoke the sentence that still lands like a stone when I remember it:

"I know that none of you… will see my face again."

They wept.

They embraced me.

They kissed me.

They were grieved most of all because of that sentence.

And I felt it too—the sorrow of leaving without certainty of return, the humility of being loved that much, the ache of knowing that even good relationships can be interrupted by obedience.

But before I left, I gave them what I could give:

a charge.

Pay careful attention to yourselves and to all the flock. The Holy Spirit made you overseers. Shepherd the church of God.

And I warned them: wolves would come, and even from among themselves people would arise, speaking twisted things. I wasn't trying to frighten them. I was trying to prepare them.

Because part of loving people is telling the truth about what can threaten them.

I reminded them of my example: how I worked with my own hands, how I coveted no one's silver or gold, how I showed them that by working hard we must help the weak.

And then I gave them the sentence that steadied me, too:

"It is more blessed to give than to receive."

Blessed.

Not safe.

Not easy.

Blessed.

Then we knelt.

We prayed.

The kind of prayer that isn't performance, because everyone is crying.

The kind of prayer that is simply hands open to God, saying: *Hold what we cannot hold. Guard what we cannot guard. Lead what we cannot lead.*

And then we parted.

Here is what I learned at Miletus:

Farewell is part of calling.

Not every season is meant to last. Not every relationship is meant to remain in the same form. Sometimes God asks you to love people deeply and then leave them without guarantee.

That hurts.

But it can also be holy.

Because it forces you to relinquish control.

It forces you to trust that God can shepherd people better than you can.

It forces you to remember that the church does not belong to you.

It belongs to God.

Later, when I wrote to believers in other places, you can hear the same tenderness in my words: like a nursing mother caring for her children, like a father exhorting and encouraging.

Love and truth together.

Not harshness disguised as conviction.

Not softness that avoids responsibility.

Love that is willing to weep.

Love that is willing to warn.

Love that is willing to bless and release.

If you are in a season of farewell—leaving a role, ending a chapter, watching a relationship change—do not assume the grief means you failed.

Sometimes grief is evidence that you loved well.

And if you are being asked to speak truth to people you care about, don't separate honesty from tenderness.

The work entrusted is not only to preach.

It is to shepherd.

To protect.

To build others up in a way that outlasts your presence.

And when you must leave, leave on your knees—placing them back into the hands that first entrusted the work.

Formation Pause

Pause here. Breathe slowly.

- What farewell are you carrying right now—spoken or unspoken?
- Where is God asking you to release control and trust Him with people you love?
- Is there truth you need to speak with tenderness—something "profitable" you've been avoiding?
- What would it look like to bless and release without bitterness?

Offer one quiet sentence:

"Lord, teach me to love well, to speak truth with tears, and to leave what I cannot control in Your hands."

Closing line:

Sometimes the work entrusted is not staying—it is blessing, warning, praying, and leaving well.

Chapter 14
Bound

When Calling Costs What You Love

(Paul tells his own story)

Chapter banner: Sometimes the Spirit leads you forward by tightening the path—making the next step feel costly, not because you missed God, but because suffering can be part of the work entrusted.

Scripture anchors: Acts 21:1–14; Romans 8:17; Philippians 3:10

After Miletus, the road turned toward Jerusalem.

The elders had wept. We had prayed. We had parted as if it were final.

And now the sea lay before us like a long, bright corridor—beautiful and indifferent to what it cost us to walk it.

We sailed from place to place: Cos, Rhodes, Patara. Ships, ports, brief conversations with strangers who became family the moment they spoke the name of Jesus.

In every city, the same pattern repeated:

We found the disciples.
We stayed a few days.

We strengthened one another.
And then we left.

There is a tenderness in that kind of travel.

The church is scattered, but it is not separate.

You can walk into a new city with no friends and still find a table where you are known.

And yet, even with that tenderness, a weight followed me like a shadow:

I was going to Jerusalem, and I didn't know exactly what awaited me there—only that it would hurt.

In Tyre we stayed seven days.

The believers there, through the Spirit, urged me not to go on to Jerusalem.

I need to say that carefully, because people misunderstand it.

They assume it means I was stubborn, refusing God's warning.

But what was happening was deeper than simple instruction.

The Spirit was revealing what awaited me.

And the believers, loving me, responded like love responds:

Don't go.

Because love doesn't want chains for someone it cares about.

Love doesn't want suffering.

Love doesn't want loss.

They weren't trying to resist God. They were trying to protect me.

And I felt the tension in my chest:

The Spirit's witness of suffering
and the community's plea for safety.

We prayed together. We knelt on the beach—men, women, children—waves rolling in, wind tugging at our clothing, tears doing what words couldn't do.

And then we parted.

Again.

We sailed to Ptolemais and greeted the brothers and sisters there.

Then to Caesarea.

And in Caesarea we stayed with Philip the evangelist—one of the seven, a man whose life already carried the marks of costly obedience. He had daughters who prophesied—women whose voices had become part of the church's life.

And while we were there, a prophet named Agabus arrived.

He took my belt.

And he did something that made the room go quiet:

He bound his own hands and feet and said, "Thus says the Holy Spirit: This is how the Jews at Jerusalem will bind the man who owns this belt and deliver him into the hands of the Gentiles."

There are moments when prophecy doesn't feel like revelation.

It feels like a blade.

Because once the future is spoken aloud, you can't pretend you didn't hear it.

Everyone in the room began to plead with me.

"Don't go."

It wasn't a polite suggestion. It was grief rising in real time. It was the human response to impending pain.

And I—standing there with my belt in someone else's bound hands—felt the cost of my calling in a way I hadn't felt it before.

It is one thing to accept suffering in theory.

It is another thing to look into the eyes of people you love and watch them break at the thought of your pain.

That is where obedience becomes sharp.

Because the question is no longer:

Do I trust God?

It becomes:

Do I love these people enough to obey even when my obedience hurts them too?

I said words that sound severe if you don't hear the tears underneath them:

"What are you doing, weeping and breaking my heart?"

Breaking my heart.

That phrase matters.

Because obedience didn't make me numb.

Calling didn't erase affection.

If anything, the longer I walked with Jesus, the more tender I became—more capable of being broken by the grief of others.

But tenderness cannot become disobedience.

So I said what I had already settled, not as bravado but as surrender:

"I am ready not only to be bound but even to die in Jerusalem for the name of the Lord Jesus."

Ready doesn't mean eager.

Ready means yielded.

Ready means: the work entrusted is worth more than my preference for safety.

And when they saw they could not persuade me, they stopped.

They said, "Let the will of the Lord be done."

That is not resignation.

It is worship.

It is the recognition that God's will is not always painless, but it is always purposeful.

And it is the only solid ground when you cannot control what comes next.

Here is what I learned in Caesarea:

Sometimes the Spirit prepares you for suffering not by removing it, but by naming it.

Sometimes God gives prophetic warning not as an exit sign, but as mercy—so you will not be surprised when the chains come.

And sometimes the hardest part of suffering is not the suffering.

It is watching what your suffering does to the people who love you.

If you are being led into something costly—if obedience is pulling you toward a road you didn't choose—pay attention to what God is doing in you *before* the trial arrives.

He may be strengthening your courage.

He may be purifying your motives.

He may be teaching you that love can hold grief without losing faith.

And if the people around you are pleading with you to take a safer path, receive their love as real—even if you cannot follow their counsel.

Sometimes community begs you to avoid the cross.

But calling asks you to trust that God is present even there.

We share in His sufferings, yes—but we also share in His life.

And if suffering is part of the fellowship, then so is hope.

Not the shallow hope that nothing will go wrong.

The deeper hope that even when it does, God will still be God.

Formation Pause

Pause here. Breathe slowly.

- Where is God leading you into something costly—not because you are being punished, but because the work entrusted requires courage?
- What warning or preparation has God already given you—so you won't be surprised later?
- How do you respond when people you love beg you to choose safety over obedience?
- What would it look like to say, with honesty and tenderness, "Let the will of the Lord be done"?

Offer one quiet sentence:
"Lord, make me ready—yielded, courageous, and faithful—whatever obedience costs."

Closing line:
Sometimes calling is not God sparing you from the chains—it is God making you ready to walk toward them with love and trust.

Chapter 15
Under the Stairs

When Calling Faces Misunderstanding

(Paul tells his own story)

Chapter banner: Not every threat comes from outsiders. Sometimes the deepest pain is being misunderstood by your own people—when fear rises, assumptions harden, and peace becomes difficult to protect.

Scripture anchors: Acts 21:17–36; Acts 22:1–21; Romans 12:18

Jerusalem welcomed me at first.

The brothers and sisters received us gladly. There were embraces, familiar faces, the relief of arrival after long travel. For a moment, it felt like rest—like I could breathe again without watching my back.

The next day we went to James, and all the elders were present.

I told them what God had done among the Gentiles through my ministry—story after story of hearts opened, households baptized, communities formed in places I never expected. As I spoke, I wasn't describing my success. I was describing God's mercy—how the gospel had leapt across boundaries and taken root.

They glorified God.

And then they spoke carefully.

"You see, brother, how many thousands there are among the Jews of those who have believed. They are all zealous for the law… and they have been told about you…"

That phrase—*they have been told*—is where trouble often begins.

Not with what is true, but with what spreads.

Rumors had grown in Jerusalem. Stories had twisted. People were saying I taught Jews to forsake Moses, to abandon circumcision, to reject the customs.

It wasn't true—but truth and rumor rarely travel at the same speed.

Fear moves faster.

And fear had already shaped the atmosphere before I arrived.

James and the elders weren't trying to trap me. They were trying to protect the fragile peace of the church in Jerusalem. They suggested a path meant to quiet suspicion: join in purification, sponsor men fulfilling a vow, show publicly that I wasn't contemptuous of the law.

So I agreed.

Not because the gospel needed proving—but because love sometimes chooses a humble path for the sake of peace.

As far as it depended on me, I wanted to live peaceably.

But peace is not always a decision one person can make.

I went to the temple.

Days passed.

And then it happened—like a spark in dry brush.

Some Jews from Asia saw me and cried out, accusing me loudly. They claimed I was teaching against the people, the law, the temple. They said I had brought Greeks into the temple and defiled the holy place.

The accusation was false, but it was believable enough to ignite anger.

The city moved fast.

Hands grabbed me. Voices rose. A crowd surged.

They dragged me out of the temple. The gates were shut behind me—like a sentence.

And then they began to beat me.

Not with careful intention.

With the wildness of a crowd convinced it is righteous.

I could feel blows landing—pain blooming across my body—while the noise thickened. People shouting, bodies pressing, rage multiplying. And in that moment I realized something I had already learned many times, but never get used to:

Some people do not want to know the truth.

They want a scapegoat.

The uproar reached the Roman tribune. Soldiers came down quickly. They pulled me out of the crowd.

And even as they rescued me, the crowd shouted one phrase over and over:

"Away with him!"

It's a chilling sound—when a mass of people wants you erased. Not corrected. Not questioned. Erased.

The soldiers brought me up the stairs toward the barracks. The crowd followed, roaring.

I was bleeding. Confused. Stunned by the speed of it all.

And still, in the middle of it, something rose in me:

Not defiance.

A desire to speak.

I turned to the tribune and asked if I might say something.

He looked at me with surprise—because people who have been beaten don't usually request a microphone.

But calling does something strange.

It makes you want to bear witness even when your body is shaking.

The tribune thought I might be an Egyptian rebel. I told him who I was—Jewish, from Tarsus, a citizen of no obscure city.

And then, standing on the steps—between the violence of the crowd and the protection of Rome—I motioned for silence.

Slowly, the noise softened.

And I spoke to them in Hebrew.

This is where the pain deepened—not because of what I suffered, but because of what I *hoped.*

I hoped that speaking their language would soften them.

I hoped that telling my story would remind them I was not their enemy.

I hoped that sincerity would matter.

So I told them who I was—how I had been raised in Jerusalem, trained under Gamaliel, zealous for God. I told them I had persecuted the Way, imprisoning and beating believers. I told them I had been sure I was right.

And then I told them what changed everything.

The light on the road.
The voice calling my name.
Jesus alive.

I spoke of Ananias—devout according to the law, well spoken of by all the Jews—laying hands on me, calling me "brother," telling me to regain my sight.

I told them I had prayed in the temple and received a vision—Jesus telling me to go, because they would not accept my testimony.

And I said the line that shattered what little peace remained:

"Go, for I will send you far away to the Gentiles."

That single word—*Gentiles*—hit the crowd like fire.

They erupted.

They shouted again:

"Away with such a fellow from the earth! For he should not be allowed to live."

They threw dust into the air. They tore at their garments. The storm returned.

And I stood there realizing something painfully clear:

Even when you speak your story honestly, people can still refuse it.

Even when you share your heart, people can still prefer their assumptions.

The tribune ordered me inside. He meant to examine me by flogging—to force the truth out of me by pain.

And there, inside, in the shadowed place under the stairs, I asked the question that shifted everything:

"Is it lawful for you to flog a man who is a Roman citizen and uncondemned?"

The room changed.

Because citizenship carried weight Rome respected, even when Rome didn't respect much else.

The tribune became afraid. The plan stopped. The immediate violence paused.

Sometimes God preserves you through means that feel strangely unspiritual—legal status, bureaucracy, the fear of consequences.

But even in that providence, I felt the deeper ache:

I was still misunderstood.

Still accused.

Still treated as danger by my own people.

Here is what Jerusalem taught me again:

You can be doing your best to live peaceably and still be caught in conflict.

You can be misunderstood and still be faithful.

And calling sometimes means standing between worlds—speaking to those who despise you, receiving protection from those who don't know you, and trusting God when no side feels safe.

If you are in a season of misunderstanding—if people have decided who you are without listening—do not rush to bitterness.

Grieve, yes.

But do not let grief become hardness.

Keep your heart open enough that God can still speak through you.

Sometimes the steps where you are bruised become the steps where you bear witness.

And sometimes the very crowd that rejects you becomes the backdrop for God's quiet protection.

Formation Pause
Pause here. Breathe slowly.

- Where are you being misunderstood right now—by people who assume motives you don't have?
- What part of your story do you keep wanting to explain, hoping it will change their view?
- How do you pursue peace "as far as it depends on you" without sacrificing obedience?
- What would it look like to trust God with your reputation—without becoming silent or bitter?

Offer one quiet sentence:
"Lord, keep my heart soft when I am misunderstood, and give me wisdom to speak truth with love."

Closing line:
Sometimes calling is not being received—it is being faithful on the steps, speaking in your own voice, and entrusting your reputation to God.

Chapter 16
Held in the Barracks

When Calling Must Endure Pressure and Keep a Clean Conscience
(Paul tells his own story)

Chapter banner: When the crowd's rage wouldn't quiet, God didn't remove me from danger—He placed me under protection long enough for truth to be spoken. Sometimes calling is sustained one hearing, one night, one breath at a time.

Scripture anchors: Acts 22:22–30; Acts 23:1–11; 2 Corinthians 1:8–10

The room inside the barracks felt colder than the street.

Not because the stones were colder, but because my body had already been warmed by violence—by adrenaline, by fear, by the raw shock of being hated so quickly.

Outside, the crowd still roared.

Inside, the soldiers watched me like I was a problem to manage.

And I kept thinking the same quiet thought:

This isn't what I expected when I said yes to Jesus.

But calling rarely gives you the version of the story you would choose.

The tribune had ordered me to be examined by flogging. It was Rome's way of extracting clarity through pain. And maybe, on some level, he believed pain could sort truth from rumor.

But when I asked about the legality of flogging a Roman citizen without trial, everything shifted.

Suddenly, my body mattered to them in a new way.

Not because they respected me.

Because they feared consequences.

The straps were loosened. The plan was stopped. The men around me became careful.

It is a strange mercy—being protected by a system that doesn't love you.

A strange providence—God using the fear of Rome to restrain the rage of Jerusalem.

The next day, the tribune wanted to know the real accusation. So he brought me before the council—the chief priests and the Sanhedrin.

I stood there, bruised and weary, looking into faces shaped by history, power, and fear.

And I began with what I had: integrity.

"Brothers, I have lived my life before God in all good conscience up to this day."

That sentence wasn't arrogance.

It was a confession of aim.

Because when your life is being questioned publicly, what you cling to is not reputation—it is conscience. The quiet knowledge of what you have sought before God.

But the high priest ordered those standing near me to strike me on the mouth.

Violence again—this time not from a mob, but from leadership.

I spoke sharply in return. Then, when I realized who had commanded it, I pulled back. I corrected myself. I refused to dishonor the office, even while enduring the injustice.

That moment exposed how quickly the heart can react when wounded.

It also exposed something else:

Calling doesn't remove your humanity.

It trains your humanity.

It teaches you when to speak, when to restrain, when to repent quickly, when to hold the line.

The council was divided—Pharisees and Sadducees. So I said what was true and central:

"I am on trial concerning the hope and resurrection of the dead."

That hope was not a tactic.

It was the center of everything.

Resurrection is the point where faith becomes collision—where kingdoms clash, where comfort is interrupted, where the future enters the present and demands response.

The moment I spoke it, the room fractured.

Voices rose. Arguments ignited. The dispute became so violent the tribune feared they would tear me apart.

So the soldiers came and took me back into the barracks.

Again.

Protected, not because I was cherished, but because Rome didn't want a riot.

And then night came.

Quiet settled over the fortress in a way it never settles over a city.

But my mind did not quiet easily.

I had wanted Jerusalem to hear me.

I had wanted my own people to understand.

Instead, the city had tried to silence me.

There are nights when discouragement feels like a second beating.

Not in the body, but in the soul.

You replay conversations. You wonder if you misspoke. You imagine alternative outcomes. You feel the weight of misunderstanding and ask if it will ever lift.

And in that night—when my body was sore and my future felt uncertain—the Lord came near.

Not in thunder.

Not with a long explanation.

With presence.

"Take courage," He said, "for as you have testified to the facts about Me in Jerusalem, so you must testify also in Rome."

Take courage.

That phrase was not scolding.

It was care.

Because courage is not something you summon once and keep forever.

Courage is renewed.

Sometimes daily. Sometimes hourly. Sometimes moment by moment.

And the promise of Rome didn't remove the danger in Jerusalem.

But it anchored me.

It reminded me that the work entrusted was not finished.

That the story was still moving.

That the interruptions—crowds, councils, barracks—were not proof of abandonment.

They were part of the road.

Later, when I wrote to the Corinthians, I tried to put language to what nights like that feel like:

"We were so utterly burdened beyond our strength that we despaired of life itself."

That's not poetry.

That's honesty.

Then I wrote what God had taught me through pressure:

“But that was to make us rely not on ourselves but on God who raises the dead.”

That is the quiet theology of the barracks.

Not a stage.

Not applause.

Just the slow, deep learning that the same God who raised Jesus can sustain you when you cannot sustain yourself.

If you are in a season where you feel hemmed in—limited, misunderstood, constrained—don’t assume you are off course.

Some callings are formed in wide-open spaces.

Others are formed behind locked doors.

And behind locked doors, God often does a hidden work:

He purifies motives.
He strengthens endurance.
He teaches reliance.
He steadies conscience.
He speaks one sentence that keeps you alive.

Take courage.

Not because circumstances are easy.

Because God is present.

And if He has more work for you to do, then no crowd—no council—no night of despair—can erase the story He is writing.

Formation Pause

Pause here. Breathe slowly.

- Where do you feel "confined" right now—held in a season you didn't choose?
- What would it look like to hold a clear conscience before God even when others misunderstand you?
- What pressure has brought you to the edge of your strength—and how might God be teaching you to rely on Him there?
- If Jesus spoke one sentence over you tonight, what do you need it to be?

Offer one quiet sentence:

"Lord, give me courage for the next step, and teach me to rely on You when I feel beyond my strength."

Closing line:

Sometimes God doesn't remove the walls—He meets you within them, and steadies you for the witness still ahead.

Chapter 17
Carried Through the Night

When Calling Is Protected by Unseen Hands
(Paul tells his own story)

Chapter banner: Sometimes God sustains the work entrusted not through a dramatic miracle, but through quiet protection—ordinary people, timely courage, and doors you didn't even know were there.

Scripture anchors: Acts 23:12–35; Psalm 121:1–8; 2 Timothy 1:7

Morning came, but the danger didn't leave.

After the night when Jesus stood near and told me to take courage, I expected the next day to feel steadier.

Instead, it revealed how deep the hostility ran.

More than forty men bound themselves with an oath. They pledged not to eat or drink until they had killed me.

That kind of vow is chilling—not because it is strong, but because it is hungry.

It feeds on certainty. It feeds on rage. It feeds on the belief that eliminating a person is the same as protecting God.

I know that mindset.

I used to live inside it.

That is part of what made this moment feel like looking into a mirror that I wished I could shatter.

They went to the chief priests and elders and laid out their plan. They would ask the tribune to bring me down to the council again—as if for more questioning. And along the way, they would ambush me.

A religious plan. A political request. A violent outcome.

Sometimes evil wears clean clothing.

And if the story ended there, I would not have survived.

But God did what He often does:

He used the courage of someone unnoticed.

My sister's son—my nephew—heard about the ambush.

We don't know how he heard. We only know that he did. And that he chose not to keep silent.

He came to the barracks and was allowed to see me. That alone was mercy—because prisoners are often treated like problems, not like people with families.

When he told me, I felt two things at once:

Fear, because the plot was real.
Gratitude, because God had not left me without warning.

I called one of the centurions and asked him to bring the young man to the tribune. The centurion agreed. The tribune took my nephew by the hand and went aside privately.

That detail stays with me: *by the hand.*

Power, for a moment, became gentle.

My nephew told him everything.

And the tribune listened.

He told the young man, "Do not tell anyone that you have informed me of these things."

Then he acted quickly.

Not with speeches.

With action.

He summoned soldiers—two hundred of them—along with seventy horsemen and two hundred spearmen. Nearly five hundred men to escort one prisoner.

If you've never been hunted, you may not understand how astonishing that is.

God built a shield out of Rome.

He used the machinery of empire—soldiers, horses, orders—to preserve a servant of the gospel.

Protection doesn't always come in a way that feels spiritual.

Sometimes it comes as logistics.

Sometimes it comes as paperwork.

Sometimes it comes as a commander deciding this isn't worth a riot.

And that night, they brought me out.

I imagine the city looked different from behind that escort—torches, armor, the heavy sound of boots. I wasn't walking into freedom. I was being moved like an object.

But even in that strange procession, I felt something holy under the fear:

I was being carried.

Not by my strength.

By providence.

We traveled through the night to Antipatris. Then the infantry returned, and the horsemen took me on to Caesarea.

And with me went a letter—official, composed, almost sterile in tone. The tribune wrote to Felix the governor, explaining the situation, framing me as a Roman citizen caught in a dispute among Jews.

I read that later and felt the irony of it.

Rome didn't understand the gospel.

But Rome could still become an instrument of God's restraint.

By the time we reached Caesarea, I was placed under guard in Herod's praetorium—kept safe until my accusers arrived.

Safe.

It's a complicated word.

I was not free. I was still a prisoner. The future was still uncertain.

But I was alive.

And in seasons like this, you learn to recognize mercy even when it comes wrapped in restraint.

Here is what I learned on that night road:

God does not always deliver you *from* danger.

Sometimes He delivers you *through* it.

And often, He does it through means you would never choose:

- a young man brave enough to speak
- a centurion willing to listen
- a commander motivated by order
- an escort formed by soldiers who don't even know your God

That is the humility of calling.

You begin to realize how little of your life you control—and how faithfully God watches what you cannot see.

Psalm says: "I lift up my eyes to the hills. From where does my help come?"

I used to read that as poetry.

Now I read it as memory.

Help came from a nephew.
From a hallway.

From a hand on a shoulder.
From a letter sealed with authority.

"The Lord will keep your going out and your coming in."

Even at midnight. Even under guard. Even when the road is lined with threats.

Later I wrote words that grew out of seasons like this:

"God gave us not a spirit of fear, but of power and love and self-control."

Not because fear never rises.

Because fear doesn't have to rule.

Power—not the power to dominate, but the power to endure.
Love—not the love that feels safe, but the love that stays faithful.
Self-control—the steadiness that refuses to panic when the plot is real.

If you are in a season where danger feels close—where anxiety has become loud, where you feel watched or threatened—don't assume God will always remove the threat immediately.

But do believe this:

He will keep you.

He will give you what you need for the next step.

And He may already be arranging protection you can't see yet—through ordinary people, quiet courage, and unexpected doors.

You are not alone on the night road.

Formation Pause

Pause here. Breathe slowly.

- Where do you feel "under threat" right now—emotionally, relationally, spiritually?
- Who has God placed near you as a quiet protector or truthful messenger?
- What would it look like to receive God's protection even when it comes through ordinary means?
- Where do you need the Spirit's gift of power, love, and self-control instead of fear?

Offer one quiet sentence:

"Lord, keep me in my going out and coming in, and teach me to trust Your unseen protection."

Closing line:

Sometimes God preserves the work entrusted through ordinary courage and unseen hands—carrying you through the night when you could not carry yourself.

Chapter 18
Two Years

When Calling Waits Without Wasting

(Paul tells his own story)

Chapter banner: Some seasons of calling are not measured in miles, but in days. Waiting can feel like loss—until you realize God is still forming you, still strengthening others, still advancing the work in ways you cannot see.

Scripture anchors: Acts 24:1–27; Acts 25:1–12; Philippians 1:12–14

Caesarea was cleaner than Jerusalem.

The air felt less volatile. The streets felt more ordered. And yet, I was still a prisoner—still held, still watched, still waiting for men in power to decide what to do with my life.

When my accusers arrived, they didn't come quietly.

They came with a lawyer.

Tertullus spoke smoothly—flattering Felix, accusing me of stirring riots, calling me a ringleader of a sect, claiming I profaned the temple. He made my life sound like a public threat.

And I stood there listening, remembering how easily a story can be shaped when the goal is not truth, but outcome.

When it was my turn, I spoke plainly.

I hadn't incited a riot. I hadn't started trouble. I hadn't desecrated the temple. I confessed what I could confess without shame:

I worship the God of our fathers, believing everything laid down in the Law and the Prophets.

And I said the one sentence that always brings the real issue into the light:

I have hope in God… that there will be a resurrection of both the just and the unjust.

That hope is never "neutral."

Resurrection implies accountability.
It implies a coming judgment.
It implies that power is temporary.
It implies that Caesar is not the final word.

So I spoke of my aim:

I take pains to have a clear conscience toward both God and man.

Conscience.

I've come back to that word again and again, because when your freedom is taken, when your future is uncertain, what remains in your custody is your soul. Your conscience becomes your private sanctuary—either a place of peace or a place of torment.

Felix listened.

He had enough knowledge of "the Way" to understand this wasn't as simple as my accusers wanted it to be. So he postponed the decision. He ordered me kept in custody, but with some liberty—friends allowed to attend to my needs.

It sounds merciful, and in some ways it was.

But mercy mixed with delay becomes another kind of trial.

Days passed.

Then Felix came again—this time with Drusilla, his wife.

And he wanted to hear me speak about faith in Christ Jesus.

People in power sometimes do that. They treat spiritual conversation like entertainment—something to sample, something to observe from a safe distance.

But the gospel doesn't stay on a tasting menu.

So I spoke the truth that love requires.

I reasoned about righteousness and self-control and the coming judgment.

Not as condemnation.

As clarity.

Because rulers are still human beings. And human beings still answer to God.

Felix became afraid.

That fear wasn't repentance. Not yet.

It was the discomfort that rises when truth gets too close to the parts of you you've protected.

So he sent me away:

"Go away for the present. When I get an opportunity I will summon you."

Opportunity.

That word can be a soft form of refusal.

"I'll deal with it later."
"Not now."
"Not when it costs me."

And then the other motive surfaced—quiet, ugly, familiar in the halls of power:

He hoped for money.

A bribe.

He sent for me often, conversed with me, keeping me near—not because he wanted salvation, but because he wanted profit.

That is a particular kind of humiliation: being kept close because someone is trying to extract something from you.

And then time stretched.

Not days.

Months.

Years.

Two years.

Two years of being held while my case remained unresolved. Two years of waking up and realizing you are still here. Two years of not knowing whether today will be the day you're released—or the day you're forgotten.

If you've never waited like that, you may not understand how spiritual it becomes.

Waiting strips you.

It removes the comfort of progress.
It exposes the parts of you addicted to productivity.
It reveals whether your identity is rooted in usefulness or in belonging to God.

Two years.

And during those two years, I had to learn a hard, holy discipline:

Do not let delay become despair.

I couldn't control Felix. I couldn't control the legal system. I couldn't force integrity into a man who preferred convenience.

But I could remain faithful.

I could pray.
I could speak when invited.
I could encourage believers who visited.
I could write.
I could keep my heart from hardening.

I began to see that waiting is not always wasted time.

Sometimes waiting is where God deepens the work entrusted.

Because the work entrusted is not only what you do.

It is also what you become.

Eventually Felix was succeeded by Festus.

And Festus, wanting favor with the Jews, asked if I was willing to go to Jerusalem to be tried there.

I knew what that meant.

A "trial" in Jerusalem would not be a fair hearing.

It would be an ambush with paperwork.

So I said what my citizenship allowed me to say:

I appealed to Caesar.

That moment wasn't pride.

It was stewardship.

It was using the means available to protect the work entrusted from being snuffed out by men who had already decided my outcome.

Festus conferred with his council and answered:

"To Caesar you have appealed; to Caesar you shall go."

That sentence landed like a door opening and closing at the same time.

Opening—because the road was moving again.
Closing—because it meant a new kind of danger.

Rome.

The empire.

The center.

And yet, I remembered what Jesus had told me in the barracks:

You must testify also in Rome.

So here is what Caesarea taught me:

Sometimes calling advances through delay.

Sometimes God leaves you in a holding pattern long enough to purify you of the need to control outcomes.

Sometimes He lets you feel the weight of "not yet" so your faith becomes sturdier than circumstance.

And sometimes, when the door finally opens, it is not into comfort.

It is into deeper witness.

If you are in a "two-year" season—maybe not literally two years, but a stretch of time that feels stalled—hear me:

Delay does not mean denial.

Being held does not mean being forgotten.

God is still with you in the in-between.

And He may be doing something in you that will become strength for someone else later.

I wrote words once that came from places like this:

What has happened to me has really served to advance the gospel.

That's not optimism.

That's testimony.

Because God can advance His work even when your life looks restrained.

Even in prisons.

Even in courtrooms.

Even in seasons when the calendar moves and your situation does not.

Formation Pause

Pause here. Breathe slowly.

- Where are you experiencing delay right now—waiting for clarity, release, resolution, or change?
- What temptation rises in you during waiting: bitterness, anxiety, striving, numbness?
- How might God be deepening your conscience, your self-control, or your trust in this "in-between" season?
- What would it look like to believe that the gospel can still advance through your restraint?

Offer one quiet sentence:

"Lord, keep me faithful in the waiting, and teach me to trust You when progress is slow."

Closing line:

Waiting can feel like loss—but in God's hands, even delay can become a doorway for the work entrusted.

Chapter 19
Before Kings

When Calling Must Stand and Speak
(Paul tells his own story)

Chapter banner: There are moments when calling is reduced to one thing: stand up, tell the truth, and trust God with the consequences. Sometimes your defense becomes a doorway for witness.

Scripture anchors: Acts 25:13–27; Acts 26:1–32; 2 Timothy 4:16–18

After I appealed to Caesar, I expected the path forward to be straightforward.

Not easy—nothing about Rome felt easy—but at least clear.

Instead, I found myself in another kind of waiting: the awkward waiting of bureaucracy trying to decide how to describe you.

Festus had inherited my case, but he didn't understand it. He could tell it wasn't the kind of criminal matter Rome usually cared about. No theft. No insurrection. No obvious crime that fit their categories.

Just disputes about religion. About words. About a man named Jesus who was dead, and whom I insisted was alive.

That sentence alone can sound small.

But everything hangs on it.

Then King Agrippa came to Caesarea with Bernice. They arrived with ceremony—purple, gold, soldiers, the subtle message of power: *we belong to the center of things.*

Festus spoke to Agrippa about my case. He admitted the problem plainly: I had appealed to Caesar, but he had nothing definite to write about me.

And that is how I found myself again in a public hearing.

Not because anyone was seeking justice.

Because they needed a summary.

It's strange, being placed before powerful people not so they can understand you, but so they can label you. Yet God has a way of using even labels as openings.

Agrippa said he wanted to hear me.

So the next day they assembled with great pomp. Commanders, prominent men of the city, the full room arranged like a stage.

And I was brought in.

The prisoner.

The accused.

The one everyone talked about, but no one could clearly explain.

Festus introduced the situation: the Jews wanted me condemned, but he found I had done nothing deserving death. Still, because I appealed to Caesar, he was sending me—he just needed something to write.

Then Agrippa turned to me.

“You have permission to speak for yourself.”

Permission.

It’s a small word, but when your life is in someone else’s hands, small words carry weight.

So I lifted my chained hands slightly and began.

I didn’t start with anger.

I didn’t start with accusation.

I started with story.

Because story has a way of slipping past defenses.

And because, if I'm honest, I wanted Agrippa to know: I am not your enemy. I am one of your people. I know our Scriptures. I know our hope.

I told him I had lived as a Pharisee—the strictest party of our religion. I told him my life was shaped by hope: the promise God made to our fathers, the hope our twelve tribes worship night and day to see fulfilled.

Then I asked the question that still feels like lightning:

"Why is it thought incredible by any of you that God raises the dead?"

That question isn't a trick.

It's the hinge.

If God is Creator, resurrection is not impossible.

If God is covenant-keeper, resurrection is not strange.

If God is faithful, resurrection is the kind of thing faith has always been reaching toward.

Then I told him the part of my story that still humbles me:

I was convinced I ought to do many things in opposing the name of Jesus.

I locked believers up. I punished them. I tried to force them to blaspheme. I raged against them.

I didn't say it to shock him.

I said it because it's true.

And because it means no one can accuse me of being lightly persuaded.

I didn't drift into this faith.

I was interrupted by it.

Then I spoke of the road to Damascus—the light brighter than the sun, the voice calling my name:

"Saul, Saul, why are you persecuting Me?"

And I told him what the voice said next—what still steadies me when everything else shakes:

"I have appeared to you for this purpose… to appoint you as a servant and witness… delivering you from your people and from the Gentiles—to whom I am sending you… to open their eyes… that they may turn from darkness to light… that they may receive forgiveness… and a place among those who are sanctified by faith in Me."

That is not ideology.

That is commissioning.

So I told Agrippa the simplest truth of my life:

"I was not disobedient to the heavenly vision."

Not because I never struggled.

Because I could not deny what I had seen.

I began to preach repentance and turning to God—first in Damascus, then in Jerusalem, then throughout Judea, and also to the Gentiles. And that was why I had been seized: not for breaking the law, but for telling people that Jesus is alive and that God calls all people to turn toward Him.

I said I was saying nothing beyond what Moses and the Prophets said would come to pass: that the Christ must suffer, and that by being the first to rise from the dead, He would proclaim light to our people and to the Gentiles.

That's when Festus interrupted me loudly:

"Paul, you are out of your mind; your great learning is driving you out of your mind."

I answered calmly, because calm is sometimes the truest strength:

"I am not out of my mind, most excellent Festus, but I am speaking true and rational words."

Then I turned toward Agrippa, because I knew he understood our Scriptures, our history, our hope.

“King Agrippa, do you believe the Prophets? I know that you believe.”

And Agrippa replied with words that can be read more than one way—half amused, half unsettled:

“In a short time would you persuade me to be a Christian?”

I didn’t pressure him.

I didn’t perform.

I said what I meant—with love and with ache:

“Whether short or long, I would to God that not only you but also all who hear me this day might become such as I am—except for these chains.”

Except for these chains.

That sentence is the shape of calling in one line.

I want you to know Christ.

I do not want you to suffer harm.

I want you to be free.

I am willing to be bound if it means you can be unbound.

When the hearing ended, Agrippa and Festus spoke privately and agreed:

“This man is doing nothing deserving death or imprisonment.”

And Agrippa added:

“This man could have been set free if he had not appealed to Caesar.”

That’s one of the strange ironies of my life.

The appeal meant Rome.

Rome meant risk.

But Rome was also part of the promise Jesus had spoken: you will testify there.

So I didn’t regret the appeal.

Because calling is not only about the fastest path to freedom.

It’s about the path God has marked for witness.

Later, when I wrote to Timothy, I described a different moment—standing in defense without friends beside me:

“At my first defense no one came to stand by me… But the Lord stood by me and strengthened me… and I was rescued from the lion’s mouth.”

That is the truest thread running through every courtroom and every hearing:

People may abandon you.

Systems may misunderstand you.

Power may mock you.

But the Lord stands near.

He strengthens.

He carries the work forward even through your restraint.

If you are in a season where you must "stand before kings"—maybe not literal kings, but authority, pressure, accusation, evaluation—remember this:

You do not need to control the room.

You need to be faithful.

Speak truth without contempt.

Tell your story without embellishment.

Hold your conscience clean.

And trust the Lord to stand by you when no one else does.

Because sometimes your defense becomes a doorway.

Not because the room is friendly.

But because God is present.

Formation Pause
Pause here. Breathe slowly.

- Where are you being asked to speak clearly under pressure—without panic, without performance?
- What part of your story is God inviting you to tell with honesty and humility?
- Who are you tempted to fear, and what would it look like to entrust the outcome to God?
- If the Lord stood beside you tonight, what courage would rise?

Offer one quiet sentence:
"Lord, stand with me when I must speak, and make my witness faithful—whether the room receives it or resists it."

Closing line:
Sometimes calling is simply this: stand, tell the truth, and trust the Lord to be present in the chains.

Chapter 20
The Storm

When Calling Holds Steady in What You Cannot Control

(Paul tells his own story)

Chapter banner: Some of the most sacred leadership I have ever offered happened with chains on my wrists and a storm over my head—when I could not steer the ship, but I could still steady souls.

Scripture anchors: Acts 27:1–44; Psalm 107:23–32; 2 Corinthians 11:25

When they decided we would sail for Italy, I was handed over to a centurion named Julius.

That detail matters, because calling often moves forward through people who do not share your faith but still choose decency. Julius treated me with a kindness I didn't expect. He didn't erase the chains, but he did not add cruelty to them.

We boarded a ship and began the long movement toward Rome.

At first, it was ordinary—ports, wind, the steady language of sailors. The sea has its own vocabulary.

You learn quickly that it doesn't care about your plans.

We made slow progress. The winds were against us. Days took longer than they should have. And eventually we arrived at a place called Fair Havens—near the city of Lasea.

It was late in the season.

Sailing had become dangerous.

Even those who love the sea know when the sea turns treacherous.

I warned them.

Not as a captain—I wasn't one.

Not as an expert sailor.

As a man who has learned to listen.

"Men," I said, "I perceive that the voyage will be with injury and much loss… not only of the cargo and the ship, but also of our lives."

But the centurion trusted the pilot and the owner more than me.

That makes sense.

People trust credentials.

They trust experience.

They trust what looks practical.

And when a gentle south wind began to blow, they believed it confirmed their plan.

So we sailed.

There is a particular kind of lesson that only comes after a warning is ignored.

Not the satisfaction of being right—calling doesn't mature through that.

The lesson is this: you can speak truth and still be overruled.

And you can still remain faithful after that.

Not long after we left, the storm arrived.

A northeaster—violent, relentless.

The kind of wind that doesn't negotiate.

The ship was caught. We couldn't face into it, so we gave way and were driven.

That phrase—*driven*—describes more than sailing.

It describes seasons of life.

Times when you are no longer steering, only enduring.

We secured the lifeboat with difficulty. We undergirded the ship, wrapping it with cables, trying to hold it together. We feared running aground, so we lowered gear. The next day we began throwing cargo overboard. The next, the ship's tackle.

When neither sun nor stars appeared for many days, and the storm continued, we finally gave up all hope of being saved.

Hope is often lost first in the sky.

When you can't see light, direction, or any sign of steadiness, the mind begins to collapse inward. The body keeps moving, but the soul starts to surrender.

For a long time no one ate.

Not because they were fasting.

Because fear steals appetite.

Weakness spreads quietly in a storm.

Then I stood.

Not to perform.

To serve.

And I said something that might sound strange from a prisoner:

"Men, you should have listened to me…"

I didn't say it to shame them.

I said it to re-open trust.

Because the moment you realize you ignored wisdom, you tend to go one of two ways:

- you harden in pride, or
- you soften into listening.

I needed them to listen now.

"Yet now I urge you to take heart," I said, "for there will be no loss of life among you, but only of the ship."

How could I say that?

Not because I felt strong.

Because God had met me.

In the night, an angel of the God to whom I belong and whom I worship stood by me and said:

"Do not be afraid, Paul… you must stand before Caesar. And behold, God has granted you all those who sail with you."

Granted.

That word stunned me.

It meant my life was not only being preserved for my own calling.

It meant the people around me were being preserved too.

Because God is not stingy with mercy.

And calling—true calling—does not shrink your heart. It expands it.

So I told them:

“Take heart… I have faith in God that it will be exactly as I have been told.”

Then I added what I couldn’t avoid:

“But we must run aground on some island.”

In other words: **deliverance would not look clean.**

The promise was life, not comfort.

Safety, not control.

We kept drifting.

Fourteen nights.

Do you know what two weeks of storm does to a human being?

It strips you down to the simplest realities: breath, hunger, fear, endurance. You stop thinking in long sentences. You think in impulses: *survive, survive, survive.*

And in the middle of that, sailors tried to escape. They lowered the lifeboat under pretense, but their real plan was to abandon the ship.

I told the centurion and soldiers:

“Unless these men stay in the ship, you cannot be saved.”

So the soldiers cut away the ropes and let the lifeboat fall.

Sometimes survival requires decisive loss.

Sometimes you must release the false escape route.

Then, as dawn approached, I urged everyone to eat.

Again, a strange thing for a chained man to do.

But leadership is not always a title.

Sometimes it is simply the willingness to care for others when everyone is afraid.

“Today is the fourteenth day,” I said, “that you have continued in suspense and without food… Therefore I urge you to take some food. For it will give you strength… not a hair is to perish from the head of any of you.”

Then I took bread.

And in front of them all, I gave thanks to God.

That moment felt like communion in a storm.

Not a church gathering.

A ship full of exhausted strangers.

But the act was the same:

gratitude offered in the middle of uncertainty.

Then I broke the bread and ate.

And they all were encouraged and ate some food themselves.

Two hundred seventy-six souls.

All strengthened by a simple act: *eat, breathe, take heart.*

Afterward, we threw the wheat into the sea.

More letting go.

More surrender.

When daylight came, we saw land but didn't recognize it. A bay with a beach. They decided to run the ship ashore.

They cut anchors loose. They loosened rudder ropes. They hoisted the foresail.

And then we struck a reef.

The bow stuck fast. The stern was broken by the pounding of the surf.

The ship was coming apart.

Soldiers planned to kill the prisoners so none could swim away.

That's what fear does—it turns protection into violence.

But Julius wanted to save me, and he stopped them.

He ordered those who could swim to jump overboard first, then the rest to follow on planks or pieces of the ship.

And just as God had promised:

We all reached land safely.

Not with dignity.

Not with a dry robe.

Not with a story that looked impressive.

But alive.

Sometimes that is the mercy.

Later I wrote, almost casually, "Three times I was shipwrecked."

People read that like a résumé of suffering.

But in the moment, shipwreck is not a line in a letter.

It is cold water.

It is salt in your mouth.

It is the sound of wood breaking.

It is the decision to trust the next plank.

And through it all, I learned again:

Calling doesn't mean you get to control the sea.

It means you learn to trust God when you can't.

You may be in a storm right now—one you didn't cause, one you can't calm.

Hear me:

You can't always steer.

But you can still be faithful.

You can still speak hope.
You can still encourage others.
You can still give thanks in the dark.

You can still eat the bread that strengthens you for the next step.

And you can believe this, even while the ship breaks:

God is present.

He stands by you in the night.

He grants mercy beyond what you asked.

And sometimes the storm does not end with a smooth landing.

Sometimes it ends with shipwreck and survival.

But survival is not small.

It is often the doorway to the next witness.

Formation Pause

Pause here. Breathe slowly.

- What storm are you in right now—where you cannot control outcomes, timing, or direction?
- Where is God inviting you to "take heart" even before the sea calms?
- What practical faithfulness would help you endure today—rest, food, honest prayer, asking for help?
- Who around you needs steady encouragement, and what could you offer without pretending you're not afraid?

Offer one quiet sentence:
"God of the storm, stand by me in the night, and teach me to take heart when I cannot see the way."

Closing line:
In the storm, calling may not steer the ship—but it can steady the souls aboard, trusting God for the shore ahead.

Chapter 21
Kindness After Wreckage

When Calling Continues on the Shore
(Paul tells his own story)

Chapter banner: After the storm, the body still trembles, the losses still ache, the future still feels uncertain. On Malta, God often meets us first through simple kindness—healing can begin with a fire and an open hand.

Scripture anchors: Acts 28:1–10; Lamentations 3:22–23; Hebrews 13:2

We reached land on broken pieces of the ship.

Planks under our arms. Salt in our mouths. Clothes heavy with seawater. Bodies shaking from cold and fear and two weeks of holding our breath against the wind.

The shore did not feel like triumph.

It felt like collapse.

When you survive something that should have swallowed you, your body doesn't immediately celebrate. It trembles. It tries to remember how to breathe without bracing. It holds grief for what was lost even while gratitude whispers, *You're alive.*

We learned the island was called Malta—an unfamiliar name, an unexpected landing, the kind of place you don't plan to arrive.

But I've learned something about God:

The places you don't plan are often the places He has prepared.

The people there met us with "unusual kindness."

That phrase still warms me.

They didn't ask who we were. They didn't ask what we had done. They didn't require proof that we deserved help. They saw wet, shaking strangers on their shore—and they built a fire.

A fire is such a small thing.

And yet when you're cold enough, it becomes salvation.

It was raining. The wind still carried bite. So they gathered sticks, made room, offered warmth.

Hospitality is holy, even when it comes from people who don't know they're participating in God's care.

I went to gather sticks too.

Old habits of work don't die easily. Even after storms, I found mysclf wanting to contribute—wanting to give my hands something useful to do.

Sometimes your hands know how to serve before your heart knows how to rest.

And then—after all that—another trial.

As I placed the bundle on the fire, a viper came out, driven by the heat, and fastened onto my hand.

The snake hung there like a sentence:

After all that, now this.

The islanders saw it and interpreted the story the way humans often do. They assumed I must be guilty—justice catching up to me.

Isn't that how quickly we explain suffering?

We want it to mean something simple:

He deserved it.
She caused it.
This is punishment.
This is payback.

It comforts people to believe pain is always earned, because then they can pretend they are safe as long as they behave.

I didn't argue.

I didn't defend myself.

I simply shook the creature into the fire—and waited.

They watched, expecting swelling, collapse, death.

But nothing happened.

And the human heart swung again—fast and extreme. If I wasn't guilty, they decided, I must be divine.

First they said, "He deserves it."
Then they said, "He's a god."

Both were wrong.

I wasn't a murderer being punished.

I wasn't a god being honored.

I was a servant being preserved.

The God who had promised Rome was still keeping His word—even on a wet shoreline with a snake and a fire.

Then kindness deepened into community.

The chief man of the island, Publius, welcomed us into his home and entertained us hospitably for three days.

Calling is so often carried by tables.

But in Publius's home there was suffering too. His father was sick with fever and dysentery—weak, wasting, the kind of illness that makes everyone in the house feel helpless.

I went in.

And I remembered again: the gospel is not an idea. It is mercy for bodies. It is compassion that steps into real rooms where people hurt.

I prayed. I laid my hands on him.

And he was healed. Not as a display—*as kindness.*

Word spread quickly. Others who were sick came and were cured. Malta became, for a season, a place where grace touched ordinary lives—through prayer, through presence, through hands that did not belong to gods or heroes, but to servants.

And when we were about to sail, they honored us greatly and put on board whatever we needed. Provision again.

Notice what God did on Malta:

He met us first with a fire.
Then with protection.
Then with a table.
Then with healing.
Then with provision for the next step.

The work entrusted did not pause because the ship broke.

It continued—through kindness.

Storms can make you forget this:

God does not only meet you with miracles and visions.

Sometimes He meets you with people who gather sticks. With strangers who build fires. With hands that pass you bread. With a home that opens for three days. With warmth when you are shivering.

And that is not "less spiritual."

It is the mercy of God arriving in a form your nervous system can receive.

Lamentations says His mercies are new every morning.

Sometimes they look like sunrise.

Sometimes they look like firelight.

Sometimes, after wreckage, the first mercy isn't an answer.

It's warmth.

And calling—calling continues right there.

Not when you feel strong again.

Not when you finally understand why the storm happened.

But when you receive kindness without suspicion, and you offer mercy without spectacle, and you let God restart your heart—one small fire at a time.

Formation Pause

Pause here. Breathe slowly.

- Where have you survived something that left you trembling—relieved to be alive, but still carrying shock and grief?
- Who has shown you "unusual kindness" on the shore—people who built a fire for you when you were cold?
- Are you quick to interpret suffering as punishment—either for yourself or for others—instead of holding it with compassion?
- What would it look like to receive hospitality as God's care, and to offer mercy from your own healing?

Offer one quiet sentence:

"Lord, meet me with Your mercy in ordinary kindness, and teach me to receive and give it freely."

Closing line:

Sometimes grace meets you first as warmth—before it becomes anything else.

Chapter 22
Rome at Last

When Calling Arrives Still in Chains

(Paul tells his own story)

Chapter banner: Sometimes the destination you longed for does not arrive as freedom. Rome came to me as custody, limitation, and waiting—yet the gospel moved forward anyway, house by house, heart by heart.

Scripture anchors: Acts 28:11–31; Philippians 1:12–14; Ephesians 6:19–20

After three months on Malta, we sailed again.

The sea was calmer, but I had learned not to confuse calm water with a simple life. Calm is a gift, but it is not a guarantee. We traveled on another ship and came to Syracuse, then Rhegium, then Puteoli.

In Puteoli, we found brothers and sisters.

Every time that happened—every time I stepped into a new place and found family—I felt the same quiet wonder:

The church is everywhere.

Not everywhere in influence.

Everywhere in presence.

Hidden like seeds, scattered through the empire, held together by a Spirit stronger than distance.

They asked us to stay seven days.

Seven days of rest in the middle of a long journey. Seven days of conversation, prayer, bread shared across a table, the kind of ordinary fellowship that heals places in the heart you didn't know were bruised.

Then we set out for Rome.

And along the way, believers came to meet us—some as far as the Forum of Appius, others to the Three Taverns. When I saw them, I thanked God and took courage.

That line is simple, but it is honest.

Courage is renewed through love.

Sometimes you don't need a new strategy.

You need a face that reminds you you're not alone.

When we entered Rome, I was allowed to stay by myself with the soldier who guarded me.

Not a dungeon.

Not freedom.

A kind of in-between: a rented place, a chain, and a constant presence beside me.

Calling arrived with restrictions.

And that was the lesson: the promise of Rome was not the promise of comfort.

It was the promise of witness.

Three days after arriving, I called together the local leaders of the Jews.

If you've followed my story, you know why.

I never stopped longing for my people. I never stopped praying they would see what I had seen.

So when they came, I spoke plainly:

"I have done nothing against our people or the customs of our fathers, yet I was delivered as a prisoner from Jerusalem into the hands of the Romans."

I told them the Romans had examined me and wanted to release me, because there was no reason for death. But the Jews objected, so I was compelled to appeal to Caesar—not because I had a charge to bring against my nation, but because I needed protection from injustice.

Then I said the sentence that has become the thread through my whole life:

"It is because of the hope of Israel that I am wearing this chain."

Hope.

Not ideology.

Hope.

Resurrection hope.

Messiah hope.

God-keeping-His-promises hope.

They told me they had received no letters about me from Judea, and none of the brothers who came reported anything bad. But they wanted to hear what I thought, because this "sect" was spoken against everywhere.

So we arranged a day.

Many came to my lodging.

And from morning until evening, I explained and testified about the kingdom of God—trying to convince them about Jesus from the Law of Moses and from the Prophets.

Some were convinced.

Some disbelieved.

That pattern followed me all the way to Rome: reception and resistance, openness and refusal.

And I felt it again—the ache of divided response.

They left disagreeing among themselves. And as they departed, I spoke one last word that was both sorrow and truth:

"The Holy Spirit was right… This people's heart has grown dull…"

Then I said what I had learned to say without contempt:

"This salvation of God has been sent to the Gentiles; they will listen."

Not as a threat.

As reality.

God's mercy doesn't stall because one group refuses it.

He keeps moving toward the receptive.

Then the story becomes wonderfully simple.

For two whole years I lived there at my own expense.

Two years.

Again.

Waiting, but not wasting.

I welcomed all who came to me, proclaiming the kingdom of God and teaching about the Lord Jesus Christ with all boldness and without hindrance.

Without hindrance.

That phrase is astonishing because I was still chained.

But the gospel was not.

Rome could limit my movements, but it could not stop the word from traveling through conversations, letters, visitors, meals, prayer.

The soldier guarding me heard it.

The people who came and went carried it.

Households were touched.

Hearts opened.

And the work entrusted moved forward—through a man who could not go anywhere.

In those years I wrote letters.

Some people call them "prison epistles," but they are more than that.

They are evidence that calling is not reduced by limitation.

It is refined.

I wrote to the Philippians—words formed in chains that still carry joy:

"What has happened to me has really served to advance the gospel."

Advance.

Not because I was free.

Because God was faithful.

I wrote of the whole imperial guard hearing about Christ, of believers becoming bolder because of my imprisonment.

Calling is strange like that.

Sometimes your restraint becomes someone else's courage.

I wrote to the Ephesians—asking for prayer, not for escape, but for boldness:

"Pray… that words may be given to me… to proclaim the mystery of the gospel… for which I am an ambassador in chains."

Ambassador.

In chains.

That is the paradox of the gospel:

You can be bound and still represent a kingdom that cannot be bound.

If you are waiting for your calling to "start" when conditions improve—when you feel freer, healthier, more resourced, more recognized—Rome will correct you.

Calling starts where you are.

Witness happens where you are.

The work entrusted continues in your actual life, not the life you wish you had.

Sometimes it looks like travel and preaching in marketplaces.

Sometimes it looks like a rented room and a chain.

But either way, God is still God.

And the gospel still moves.

Formation Pause

Pause here. Breathe slowly.

- Where do you feel restricted right now—limited in freedom, energy, time, resources, or opportunity?
- What would it look like to believe the gospel can still advance through your limitations?
- Who might God be bringing "to your door"—people you can welcome, encourage, teach, or love right where you are?
- What would boldness look like for you today—not loudness, but faithful clarity?

Offer one quiet sentence:

"Lord, teach me to be faithful where I am, and let Your work continue through me even in limitation."

Closing line:

Rome did not remove the chains—but it could not hinder the gospel.

Chapter 23
The Work Entrusted

When Calling Becomes Legacy
(Paul reflects, near the end)

Chapter banner: In the end, calling is not measured by how much you accomplished, how far you traveled, or how many heard your name. It is measured by whether you were faithful with what was placed in your hands.

Scripture anchors: 2 Timothy 4:6–8; Acts 20:24; Philippians 3:12–14; Hebrews 12:1–2

I do not know how many more years I will be given.

I have learned not to demand that knowledge.

There was a time when I thought calling meant momentum—movement, cities reached, letters written, churches planted. And those things mattered. They still matter.

But now, with chains familiar to my wrists and time no longer feeling endless, I see the work entrusted more clearly.

Calling was never about my reach.

It was about my faithfulness.

From the beginning, I was given something precious and dangerous: the gospel of Jesus Christ. Not an idea to debate, not a system to control, not a reputation to defend—but a life to bear witness to.

I was entrusted with a message that would cost me comfort, certainty, safety, and eventually my freedom.

And I was entrusted with people.

That part surprised me.

I thought I was sent to preach.

I didn't realize I was sent to love.

To stay.
To leave.
To correct.
To encourage.
To weep.
To warn.
To trust God with people I could not protect.

The work entrusted required my voice—but also my hands, my tears, my endurance, my willingness to keep going when outcomes were unclear.

I chased perfection once.

I chased certainty.

I chased righteousness as something I could achieve.

Jesus interrupted all of that.

He did not give me a flawless path.

He gave me Himself.

And in Him, I learned that calling is not proven by absence of suffering.

It is proven by obedience within it.

I have been misunderstood by crowds and opposed by leaders.

I have been protected by strangers and betrayed by friends.

I have known moments of boldness and nights of despair.

I have been lifted by community and confined by chains.

And through it all, one truth has remained steady:

The Lord stood by me.

Not only when I was strong.

Especially when I was weak.

I once wrote words that people quote now, but they were not written from comfort:

"I have fought the good fight, I have finished the race, I have kept the faith."

That is not a boast.

It is a quiet accounting.

I did not finish because I was flawless.

I finished because I did not quit.

Because when I fell, I returned.

When I doubted, I prayed.

When I was afraid, I remembered the One who called me.

Calling does not ask you to be extraordinary.

It asks you to be faithful.

Faithful when you are celebrated.
Faithful when you are ignored.
Faithful when doors open.
Faithful when they close.
Faithful when the work feels fruitful.
Faithful when it feels hidden.

There were seasons when the work entrusted looked like crowds and conversions.

There were seasons when it looked like one conversation, one letter, one rented room, one chain.

Do not despise either.

God uses both.

I ran hard.

But I did not run alone.

Others carried the work with me—Timothy, Titus, Luke, Priscilla, Aquila, unnamed believers whose courage never made it into letters but shaped the church all the same.

If this story has taught you anything, let it be this:

You do not carry calling by yourself.

And you are not the center of it.

Jesus is.

He is the One who calls.
He is the One who sustains.
He is the One who completes what He begins.

When your strength fades, He remains.

When your understanding breaks, He holds.

When your work feels unfinished, He is not finished.

So I leave you with what I have learned—not as instruction carved in stone, but as testimony shaped by grace:

Run your race.

Not mine.

Not someone else's.

Yours.

Lay aside the weight that entangles you—not just sin, but fear, comparison, bitterness, and the need to prove yourself.

Fix your eyes on Jesus.

Not on outcomes.
Not on applause.
Not on legacy as the world defines it.

If there is a crown, it is not for those who looked impressive.

It is for those who loved His appearing.

Who trusted Him.

Who stayed faithful.

The work entrusted to me is now carried by others.

And the work entrusted to you is already in your hands.

You do not need to rush it.

You do not need to perfect it.

You only need to be faithful with it—today.

Final Formation Pause

Pause here. Sit quietly.

- What work has God entrusted to you—not in theory, but in your actual life?
- Where have you been tempted to measure your calling by outcomes instead of faithfulness?
- What would it look like to run your race with endurance, without comparison?
- If you were to offer your life back to God today, what would you say?

Offer one final sentence:

"Lord, help me to be faithful with the work You have entrusted to me, until the end."

Closing line:

Calling is not about how the story looks when it is told—it is about faithfulness while it is being lived.

Scripture Reference Index

Chapter 2: Acts 9:30; Galatians 1:17–24; Acts 11:25–26; Philippians 3:7–11

Chapter 2: Acts 11:19–30; Acts 12:25; Acts 13:1–3; Galatians 2:1–2

Chapter 2: Acts 13:13; Acts 15:36–41; Colossians 4:10; 2 Timothy 4:11

Chapter 6: Acts 15:40–41; Acts 16:6–10

Chapter 7: Acts 16:16–34; Philippians 1:12–14; Philippians 4:4–7

Chapter 8: Acts 17:1–15; 1 Thessalonians 2:1–12; 1 Thessalonians 3:1–5

Chapter 9: Acts 17:16–34; 1 Corinthians 9:19–23; 1 Thessalonians 3:1–6

Chapter 10: Acts 18:1–18; 1 Corinthians 2:1–5; 1 Thessalonians 3:6–10; 2 Corinthians 12:9–10

Chapter 11: Acts 18:18–28; Acts 19:1–10; 1 Corinthians 3:5–9; 1 Corinthians 16:19; Romans 16:3–4

Chapter 12: Acts 19:11–41; 1 Corinthians 15:9–10; Ephesians 6:10–12

Chapter 13: Acts 20:1–38; 2 Corinthians 2:1–4; 1 Thessalonians 2:7–12

Chapter 14: Acts 21:1–14; Romans 8:17; Philippians 3:10

Chapter 15: Acts 21:17–36; Acts 22:1–21; Romans 12:18

Chapter 16: Acts 22:22–30; Acts 23:1–11; 2 Corinthians 1:8–10

Chapter 17: Acts 23:12–35; Psalm 121:1–8; 2 Timothy 1:7

Chapter 18: Acts 24:1–27; Acts 25:1–12; Philippians 1:12–14

Chapter 19: Acts 25:13–27; Acts 26:1–32; 2 Timothy 4:16–18

Chapter 20: Acts 27:1–44; Psalm 46:1–3; 2 Corinthians 4:8–9

Chapter 21: Acts 28:1–10; Lamentations 3:22–23; Hebrews 13:2

Chapter 22: Acts 28:11–31; Philippians 1:12–14; Colossians 4:2–4

Chapter 23: John 17:4; 2 Timothy 4:6–8; Philippians 1:20–21; Acts 28:30–31

About the Author

Cindy H. Carr, D.Min., MACL, has spent her vocational life walking alongside people in the slow, often unseen work of formation and change. Her career has been intentionally bi-vocational, shaped by years of pastoring, business leadership, and pastoral counseling—always with a focus on helping people live with greater clarity, dignity, and wholeness.

She earned a Master of Arts in Church Leadership from Eastern Mennonite Seminary and completed her doctoral work at Liberty University. Over the years, she served multiple churches in Virginia's Shenandoah Valley in a variety of pastoral and leadership capacities.

In this season of life, Cindy's work has shifted from direct leadership into writing and education. Through her books, she helps readers implement formation-based principles she has taught throughout her career—practices centered on identity, connection, return, and steady growth without shame.

Learn more about Cindy and her work at **CindyHCarr.com**

www.ingramcontent.com/pod-product-compliance
Lightning Source LLC
LaVergne TN
LVHW010654110826
845149LV00014B/3092